D0311724

A LIFE AMONG
ANTIQUES

A LIFE AMONG ANTIQUES

Arthur Negus Talks to Bernard Price

Hamlyn
London · New York · Sydney · Toronto

Hamlyn

Published by
The Hamlyn Publishing Group Limited
London · New York · Sydney · Toronto
Astronaut House, Feltham, Middlesex
England

© Copyright
Arthur Negus 1982

First impression 1982

ISBN 0 600 34228 X

Printed in Great Britain

Contents

Foreword   7

CHAPTER ONE
How it all Began   9

CHAPTER TWO
The Young Antique Dealer   19

CHAPTER THREE
The Arm of the Law   33

CHAPTER FOUR
Poacher Turned Gamekeeper   61

CHAPTER FIVE
Antiques – Knockers and
Reflections   75

CHAPTER SIX
Going for a Song   94

CHAPTER SEVEN
On the Road   133

CHAPTER EIGHT
Home and Away   153

Index   167

Acknowledgments   168

Foreword

SINCE 1965 I have had the privilege and the pleasure of working with Arthur Negus on many hundreds of occasions; on radio and television, and on stage and the lecture platform. Like millions of others I too have been charmed and entertained by his blend of knowledge and avuncular manner. Having worked with Arthur so closely during his broadcasting career, I found myself becoming increasingly interested in the sixty-two years that had preceeded his overnight success in television's *Going for a Song*.

In 1979 I talked with Arthur about his life in a television programme I called *Arthur Negus: A Life Among Antiques*. To me it seemed the perfect title, for I am sure that Arthur Negus and antiques are entirely synonymous in the public mind, and it was because of that programme that this book materialised. What has resulted was gleaned from recordings I made with Arthur at his home, at his office, and from my notes. So far as is possible I have retained Arthur's own words in his highly individual patterns of speech. People who have enjoyed so many years of listening to Arthur Negus will no doubt take pleasure in recognising his voice in the chapters that follow.

This book undoubtedly portrays a happy man with a story well worth the telling. Arthur's knowledge and understanding of antiques, and of furniture in particular, was won the hard way, through a lifetime of personal experience. While ever patient with those who wish to learn what he has to impart, he gives but short shrift to fools and pretence in any form. Constantly described as an expert, he will have none of it. 'All I have ever said,' he will say, 'is that I like furniture.'

Arthur has now become what might well be termed a folk figure, recognised wherever he goes, welcomed at cottage or mansion. When visiting country houses that are open to the public, I have so often heard their guides take pleasure in pointing out the particular pieces of furniture that Arthur Negus liked when he was last there! If, in reading this book, you find yourself beginning to look at the objects about you with a fresh interest, then Arthur and I will be well pleased.

BERNARD PRICE

Chapter One
How it all Began

So FAR AS I CAN REMEMBER, it was late in 1964 when my secretary made an appointment for me to see a producer from the BBC, and at that time I had not the slightest idea what he wanted to see me about. The firm of auctioneers I worked for in Gloucester had in the past received several calls from various BBC people saying that they had been brought down from London, or some other region, to do a two-year stint in Bristol. Most of these callers wanted to find a knee-hole desk or a gate-leg table, or some such thing, so I really didn't pay very much attention to this latest call. I should have done, for I was soon to find out that it was about a very different matter altogether. The producer was John Irving, who, incidentally, proved to be the grandson of Sir Henry Irving, the famous actor. He said that he had an idea for a programme on antiques in which he thought I could take part. I asked him precisely what he meant by a programme on antiques. What would he want me to do? He said he thought I could go to the studio and answer some questions on antiques, but I told him I couldn't possibly do such a thing, so that seemed to be the end of that and I promptly forgot all about it.

Some three or four months later, John Irving came back to me and said that he had still got this idea of a television programme in his mind. He had made a lot of enquiries in various towns, such as Bath, Oxford, Bournemouth, Cardiff and Birmingham. While talking to various dealers somehow or another my name always seemed to crop up in the conversation, and so he had come back more than ever convinced that I could answer questions on antiques. Once more I said no because I still really had no idea of what he really wanted from me. It seemed to me I might be put into a dock or some such stand, and be cross-examined as to when George Hepplewhite was married, or how many children Chippendale had, and I thought I'd have to say, 'don't know' too often. He then told me that he had put his idea to the programme organisers in London, and they too apparently thought it might make good entertainment. He asked if I would take part in just one, a single recording, just so that he had got something in the 'can' as he put it. This recording could then be shown to the various BBC regions to see whether or not there was anything of real interest in it at all. So that was how I was persuaded to consent to go down to Bristol to take part in one programme, and he agreed to the one and only condition I made, simply that it was never to be shown.

I still felt that I would not be able to do what was wanted, and although I didn't mind making a fool of myself in front of perhaps ten or twelve people in the studio, directors, camera men and the like, I certainly wasn't going to advertise the fact that I was an ignoramus answering questions before a few million. The BBC also agreed, and I finally went down to the studio and took part in a programme which proved to be nothing like answering the sort of questions I had imagined, absolutely just the opposite. Certain objects were passed around at this recording for me to identify, and it seemed I was well able to cope with them, but the BBC of course have never shown that original recording of *Going for a Song* and I don't suppose they ever will. Soon afterwards came a BBC contract, two foolscap sheets which requested me to take part in the first and last of the six programmes they now intended to make. I was more than a little bucked about this, because it transpired that I was the only person asked to go on the first and last programme. Everyone else who was to take part, I discovered, had been invited once only, but I managed somehow or another to get myself in on the first and last. Eventually the great day came when this programme went out live I had not the slightest idea whether it was good or bad, but a man came along to me in the studio when it was all over and put his hand on my shoulder and said, 'Not bad, not bad at all, are you free to come next week?' I said, 'Yes, of course,' and so again I did another programme, which afterwards produced the same man saying the same things, and so I went again and produced programme number 3. That was how it all proceeded. In the whole of the ten years that the programme ran, although not continuously, I only missed two recordings during one summer when my wife and I were away on holiday. So that's the story of how *Going for a Song* began and it's rather remarkable, I think, that although I've taken part in many other programmes, if ever I am recognised and stopped in the street by complete strangers, they all refer to *Going for a Song*.

I will have more to say about *Going for a Song* and other programmes later, but the question I've been most often asked is: how did I start? You see, I was well past my sixtieth birthday when *Going for a Song* began, and apart from my own circle of friends and acquaintances nobody had ever heard of Arthur Negus until then. So, if I'm going to tell this story properly, perhaps it would be best if I started at the very beginning.

I don't know a great deal about my family history but I know as a very tiny child I was taken to see my grandfather in the little village of Godmanchester, about two miles out of Huntingdon, and my father was born in Godmanchester. What happened then is all a bit hazy in my mind but I understand he was apprenticed to a firm of cabinet makers in Huntingdon. How long he stayed with them I have no idea but as far as my memory serves me, he went to Reading in 1900 and was employed with a firm called Silver's who had premises in Duke Street, Reading. They employed fifteen or twenty cabinet makers and upholsterers and were, in those days, quite a big firm. Another thing I remember well was how he came to give notice to Silver's.

He was sent by Silver's all over the country inlaying doors. It seemed to be a fashionable thing in late Victorian or early Edwardian times for nice mahogany panelled doors to be inlaid with Grecian figures in satinwood, and he was sent away from his home by this firm for as long as three months on end and this is really what made him eventually decide to leave the firm and open a small shop in King's Road, Reading. To anyone who knows Reading the little shop is still there, right by the bridge over the river Kennet in King's Road.

I was born in 1903 and he had that little shop then. He used to tell me how Mr and Mrs Rufus Isaacs, later Lord and Lady Reading, came into that small shop and bought small pieces of furniture about the time I was born. Eventually he left King's Road and moved into Minster Street. Minster Street is practically in the centre of the town, and we lived there until he died at the very early age of fifty-three. He was a very humble man, and money was very scarce in those early days. When I was about thirteen he managed to send me to Reading School, he got a bursary, because he had been in Reading long enough to apply for one from the Local Authority, and I think he had to pay £12 a year for me to go there, a marvellous old school. I'd say my father was an unusual sort of chap, for one thing he seemed to have no interest whatsoever in making money. That's a curious thing to say, but his whole life was centred in the workshop. He had no wish to go and give £10 for a chair and sell it for £12. He'd much rather have somebody bring in a nice piece of furniture if it was damaged for him to repair, or a chair, all rickety, so he could knock it all to pieces and put it together and make it sound again.

One example which sticks in my mind, I'll never forget it, was when I came home from school one day and he said 'Sonny', I was an only child and my parents always called me 'Sonny'. 'Sonny,' he said, 'just look at this, how do you like that?' It was a mahogany tallboy I was looking at. Well I didn't know what I was looking for, of course, and I just said, 'Very nice.' 'Yes,' he said, 'but look at those canted corners.' They were a bit chipped, he had obviously repaired the tallboy but he didn't like those chipped canted corners when he had finished it. Anyway, the next day when I came home from school he called 'Come and have a look at the tallboy now.' It was all in boards, he had taken the top all to pieces, the next day he put new canted corners down the sides of the tallboy and had reconstructed the whole thing, it looked absolutely marvellous. When it went back home to its owners not a word of all the work involved was said to anyone, £3 had been the estimate for restoring it and £3 was the bill they received.

Another thing that showed what sort of chap he was, happened when talking pictures first came to Reading and we queued for an hour and a half to get into see the wonderful things that were going to appear. A man stood on the stage, and then disappeared, and reappeared on the screen and talked to us from the screen. Somebody threw a bag of flour over him in the picture and he came out of the screen, still on the stage, and with flour all over him. I'd never seen anything like it, it was absolutely fantastic. Walking home my father said, 'I've thought how I'm going to do that dresser.' He had not been looking at this wonderful invention of the cinema, his mind was going over a difficult bit of work he had to do on a dresser. 'I've thought how I can do that,' he said.

Physically he was about my height, but very different to me now, he was quite a slim man, he had a moustache and I don't think he smoked. He was always in his workshop, always working from morning until late at night. I don't know whether anyone has had experience of a glue pot boiling dry, but believe me, when an old-fashioned glue pot boils dry the smell and the stench goes all over the house, and then my mother would shout, 'Father, your glue pot's gone dry!'

As I have said, I went to Reading School and left there in 1920 to join my father in the business. It's curious the questions that I get asked now. People ask if I had any idea when I started with my father if I was going to become a personality on televison, now isn't that ridiculous? There was no TV then and most sons I think usually enter their father's businesses with no real thought about what's going to happen in the next forty or fifty years. There were only three or four pieces of furniture in the shop at that time, they were certainly old though there really wasn't much in the way of stock but, my God, in the workshop there certainly was some work, stacks of work. He worked at it all steadily and I would be longing to do something; not just standing and watching him, but all he said was, 'You just watch me and you'll be able to do it if you have to.' 'Watch me', he would say, time and time again. 'Now, you see that drawer, the way that's made, they didn't make drawers like that in the eighteenth century so this one is later. Now get under there, can't you see it's been altered, it's been altered from a washstand. Look at this dressing table, it's been turned into a knee-hole desk.' I didn't pay much attention to this, of course, I just said 'yes' and I realise now that what he was telling me was eventually to be of some great use to me. All of it was a great help, particularly in identifying old things that had been altered.

I would imagine some people would say that my mother was already old when I was born. I think she was about thirty-five, shorter than my father, and she was a quiet woman who really had the rough end of it all. I hadn't better get too involved with women in this sense, but in those days, say 1912 to 1920 and later, when one rented a little shop with living rooms over, there was no bathroom, none of the conveniences we take for granted today. My father had taken the room that was the kitchen for his workshop, so a kitchen had to be made upstairs. It was just the same, more or less, when I married, because there again my wife had to contend with all the same sort of problems until we eventually moved. My mother was always interested in the sort of work that my father was doing in the sense of a wife-husband relationship, but I don't think that either she or I realised what a really great cabinet maker he was. As the years went by he did make some very fine things, and he copied like most good cabinet makers copied, say, a Sheraton sideboard, or a Chippendale chair. We had one customer who must have had eight or ten things made specifically for himself by my father. Later, after my father had died and I had married and was living over the shop, a man called and said, 'Have you got anything your father made?' I said 'Yes, we have a sideboard upstairs' so the man said, 'I know that sideboard, I'll give you £100 for it', and £100 in 1928 or thereabouts really was money. So I ran up to my wife and said, 'I've got a madman downstairs, he wants to give £100 for our sideboard, it's not worth anything like that money.' We could have done with the money too, but she obviously had got more sense than I for she said, 'Look, if that sideboard goes out, I go out,' so I told the man that we wouldn't sell. How right she was, because we still have that sideboard, and now circumstances have altered a bit from those days I wouldn't part with it for anything. It's a beautiful sideboard, beautifully made, and there can be no deceit in it because, underneath, its got the words 'made by Arthur G. Negus'.

Those who know Reading will recall the corner of Minster Street and Chain Street, where the old shop was. It adjoined the parish church so the parish church saw all of our activities all through our lives, in Reading. I was a choirboy then, a server too. I went five times to church on a Sunday. We were married there, and had our two daughters christened there! Everything happened in St Mary's Church. Now they have pulled down nearly all the adjoining houses in Hosier Street, made walkabouts, built some offices and a huge market precinct in St Mary's Butts, so there are very few parishioners. I have gone back and had a look at it all, and it disturbs me to think that when I was in the choir that church was three-parts filled on Sundays, both morning and evening. We used to have an Evensong every night at 6 o'clock, every night a sung Evensong, and now there is nothing surrounding the old church except offices. There are daughter churches, and I understand they are well attended but poor old St Mary's Church, the parish church, stands completely isolated and really with no congregation.

I played all sorts of games. For years I played soccer, I didn't play much rugby although rugby was played at school. I took part in a certain amount of cricket, and was the school scorer at Reading school which I liked very much indeed, and I enjoyed playing tennis. I am still very interested in all manner of sports. I also played a great deal of snooker, very much more snooker than perhaps I should have done.

The subjects I most liked at school were mathematics, without doubt I could do mathematics, they didn't bother me at all. It used to be the custom in the olden days to mark everything in the shop with a private mark or code and I could add up the private marks without having them translated into figures. I did logarithms and trigonometry and particularly liked algebra. If you care to ask me what I couldn't do, I couldn't do French dictation, but I used to do my best. At school everyone had to pass their written work to the boy on their left, who marked it for you, and then every word that was wrong had to be shouted out to the master. So they started with Anderson, in alphabetical order, Anderson 5, so and so 3, and eventually the master would get into the Ns, Negus 61; I couldn't understand it, they didn't pronounce the last letter and it messed me up completely. I had no idea how to do French dictation, and the name of French cabinet makers still give me trouble today.

I am pleased that I still have friends from that school period, 1914–1920. I joined the Old Readingentsions on leaving, which is The Old Boys, and by the sheer weight of years I eventually became their President for one year, sitting at the top table at the Old Boys dinners. There are still about six or eight men that I knew as school fellows still attending those dinners. It's interesting to meet boys who on leaving school have become Old Readingentsions, where chaps of about thirty years of age will come up to me at a dinner and say, 'my name is so and so, and you knew my father'.

I remember at home in the kitchen we had four Georgian chairs, they were Regency chairs and, as they were broken by myself or by other boys who were in the kitchen with me, they were thrown away because they were worth so little and not worth repairing. No, we hadn't got many nice pieces of furniture in those early days, but we had a happy home, warm and comfortable and with plenty to eat.

We didn't go short for anything but I never had any feeling that we as a family had got any money. Yet my father always produced it when required. He was old fashioned enough not to trust banks, but there were various anxious cries at different times of 'I've lost my wallet,' and that would really cause consternation, and it would be a case of all hands on deck while we searched for it. My father naturally wore old clothes when working, but another funny thing he would do was when he perhaps tore his trousers on a nail, or a saw. He used to stick together the tear with a piece of webbing, the webbing you upholster chair seats with, he glued that underneath the tear, and eventually, after six or eight tears, he really looked as though he had spikes coming out all over his trousers because the webbing had stiffened and poked through. I got on very well with my father, I wasn't restricted in any way; they were good parents to me and nothing was too much trouble for either of them, there is no doubt about that. I was seventeen when my father died.

Chapter Two
The Young Antique Dealer

MY MOTHER MUST HAVE WONDERED what on earth the future held for us, certainly I did, but soon I was beginning to imagine myself as an antique dealer. The first thing I thought was how marvellous it was to have a cheque book and I shall never forget that, for some reason I couldn't wait to write a cheque, I so wanted to show off with it although I can't think why. I remember so vividly standing in the shop and wishing that someone would call by, anything so that I could write a cheque for I'd never written one in my life. Eventually a man did come in and said, 'Do you buy old tables?' 'Yes', I said, and followed him down to his house. It was a nice oak table and I offered him £15 for it, which he said he'd take. I flashed my cheque, wrote it, gave it to him, and carried the table back through the streets of Reading and proudly put it in the shop window. I fetched my mother and said, 'Now can you understand how we are going to get a living? We are going to live by buying and selling old bits of furniture. There's no money in all that cabinet work, and I can't do it, this is how we are going to do things now. I've just given £15 for that table and you wait and see what I get for it.' Well, she lived long enough, because it took me seven years to sell and then I sold it for £1, it must have been a dark afternoon or something. I was glad to see the back of it, biggest fake of course

19

anyone could ever imagine. There were so many set-backs, but at least I was beginning to learn.

It's an extraordinary thing but at that time when I was left on my own with no knowledge, and let it be clearly understood, no knowledge at all and only a few pounds, how many dealers quite knowingly and willingly gave me a helping hand. Many times I was stopped by one of them and told, 'Look son don't buy that, because that's dead wrong' or 'You can give another £1 or £2 for this because this is a nice article.' I used to like glass and a very well-known dealer in London, a very important man in the glass world when he died, would ring me up about sales in or around Reading. I would phone him back and say, 'There is a very nice pair of glass table lights that I should think are worth about £25.' I think he knew enough of me to trust that I would know if they were genuinely old, so he used to say, 'Well, if they are like you say I'll hold you blameless, but I'll give you £90 for them.' So that kind of thing helped tremendously and it certainly widened my knowledge about table lights.

I shall never forget when I was called to a house in Reading, and was asked if there was anything in the house that I could buy. It looked hopeless for there were only a few pieces of toilet ware on a table, and I said 'I'm afraid there's nothing here.' I was asked to look upstairs but there was nothing there either. Coming down the stairs which jutted sideways into a little kitchen, I suddenly noticed a blue lustre jug in among the toilet ware, and I said, 'I'll buy that little jug'. 'Oh you can,' I was told, and I bought it for £1. I immediately rang up the London glass dealer and said, 'I've got a blue silver-resist lustre jug I thought you might like, it's as though it's brand new.' He said, 'Well how can I see it?' Don't worry about that, I said, I'm coming up to London.' So I got on the train, in those days if one left Reading after five o'clock at night the ticket was half-a-crown return to London on what we called the theatre train. When I arrived with the jug he said, 'Isn't that nice, what do you want for it?' 'I don't know, I really don't know what it's worth.' 'Well what did you hope to get for it?' I said, '£15.' He said, 'Oh no I couldn't do that, that wouldn't be right, it's worth about £30 to me' and he gave me the money there and then. Now you meet people like that and through them you learn a lot, and they don't begrudge you a few pounds, and the self same thing happened in my dealings in furniture with different dealers. Once, for 17 shillings, I became the proud owner of what looked like a sugar basin, a little glass bowl, I thought it was old and when I got it home my mother washed it and the glass turned almost white, but as it dried it cleared and became just clear glass again. Well, we put it in the shop window and it was marked 30 shillings. It stayed there for some long time, and by long time I mean about two years, and then at last somebody came in and enquired about it. I said, 'It's ridiculous, every time you wash that bowl it goes practically white.' The fellow said, 'How much is it?' I asked him 30 shillings and he bought it. Of course, since then I've learned that is what happens to the very early glass made by George Ravenscroft, who I think had a little workshop at Wargrave. Now Shiplake, where I bought the bowl is next door to Wargrave and, ever since then I've always thought, although it has never been proved, that what sat in my window for so long was in fact a seventeenth-century piece of very rare Ravenscroft glass.

One thing I know I owned was a grandfather clock. Starting off at seventeen with few plans and no knowledge, and again bear in mind the no knowledge part, I saw a grandfather clock which I liked the look of. It was in a marquetry case, and I offered £25 for it which was accepted. I brought it back to the shop and the thing was so worn away on the base it wouldn't stand upright by itself. It had to be tied, tied at the back of the shop with a piece of string, and there it stood. I thought to myself, well, I don't suppose this will be easy to sell for the blessed thing couldn't stand up for itself at all. A dealer came in and asked, 'How much is the clock?' I said '£27.10s and he said, 'O.K. I'll have that.' So I made 50 shillings profit which was quite nice. Some months after that a man came in and said, 'I saw a clock you sold recently.' I said, 'Did you?' 'Yes,' he said, 'as a matter of fact I bought it, I'm interested in clocks. Did you notice if there was a name on the dial?' 'No', I said. 'Well there is,' he said, 'the name is printed in Latin, Edwardus East.' I've since discovered that Mr Edward East was clockmaker to Charles II and if you search for an Edward East clock today you'd better start getting on the job quickly, because it will probably take you twenty years before you even have the opportunity of buying one. Well, I had one of those you see and managed to get the great sum of 50 shillings profit. That is how it all went on, you buy things too cheaply in ignorance and sell them too cheaply in ignorance. At the same time you also give a bit too much when buying things in houses and then have to sell them at a loss. All the time you try and remember what on earth it is you are doing, and after about five or ten years you begin to get a feeling for and a smattering of knowledge about the particular works of art which you like, which in my case was furniture.

Many people who have businesses no doubt can recall some quite amusing incidents that may have happened to them. One I remember concerns a man who came in my shop wanting to sell four pewter plates. You will recall earlier in this book I spoke about my associations with St Mary's Church, and I just offered this man £1 each for the plates, which he accepted, so I gave him the £4. I sold them for £6 to another dealer in the town and about three days after that the police called. They wanted to know if I had bought any pewter lately. I told them that I had bought four plates. 'That's what we want,' they said, 'they've been stolen from a church.' Oh dear! So they called on my friend whose business was also in Reading, and took possession of the plates. I had made £2 profit, he'd lost £6, but eventually I gave him the £2 back, and we did share the loss, losing £2 each. It's extraordinary when I think back, how with all those associations with St Mary's, that I should go and buy four pewter plates like that.

Another thing I well remember was that I once had my eye on two stone lions which were sitting, or lying, on the top of Wellsteads building in the main street of Reading. Many years ago the firm were erecting a new shop front and I wondered what might happen to those two stone lions. I contacted the foreman on the site, and he said, 'They're scrap.' 'I could do with those,' I said, 'if you can get them down', and he said 'Oh they'll come down, of course.' Eventually I found them lying on the ground, I found the foreman again and gave him £20 for the two lions. Then came the question of getting them into my shop. I'd only got a hand truck in those days and they were too heavy for that, but I did find a man who had a tip-cart, a corporation tip-cart, and I suggested he might help me move one of these lions, to my shop. He said he couldn't do it then but wouldn't mind coming back in the dinner hour. So, I arranged to give him £1 and at 1 o'clock he arrived with his horse and tip-cart, and I arrived with about six other men. After a long struggle we did get a stone lion on the back of the tip-cart, when to everyone's astonishment up went the horse into the air. Poor horse, still held by the shafts and with all four legs working in mid air. The man ran round and hung on to the horse's head and just balanced it, and down came the horse. Afterwards the man turned on me and said 'That's what comes of being dishonest, working in the guvnor's time.'

Of course, you realise that over these years I was limited in the first place to going to sales within about eight or nine miles from Reading on a bicycle. Later we did manage to get some sort of a motor cycle, and then a tiny car. When I was twenty-one my mother bought me a little bull-nosed Morris Cowley which cost £199.10s. I shall never forget that little purring motor car which allowed me to go to much greater distances.

At this time I formed a friendship with a man named Harold Brown who had taken over his father's business and was much about the same age as myself. I came to an arrangement with him that I would view all the sales south and west of Reading and he would do all the sales east and north of Beaconsfield. At about 11 o'clock at night I would ring Beaconsfield 54, I've never forgotten it, 'Any good Harold?' I would ask, 'No, nothing this way, anything your way?' 'No.' 'What were the chairs like in Newbury?' 'Nine no good at all, they are repros.' 'Well I'll pick you up in the morning', he said, and in the morning he came over in his car and away we went off down the Bath Road. I asked him where we were going and he said, 'We're going to Newbury.' I said, 'I viewed that sale, those chairs are no good. There were nine Chippendale chairs all standing on cabriole legs with claw and ball feet.' 'Six are absolutely dead right,' said Harold, 'but three are reproductions.' Now I had walked in there and picked up one wrong one and like a fool came out of the house, without looking at any of the others. So we went to the sale, and in those days they used to sell chairs at so much per chair and for 57/6d each we jointly became the owners of the nine Chippendale chairs, six of which were genuine and three were reproductions ('right' and 'wrong' as they're often described in the trade). We didn't want the wrong ones, so we said to a woman who I'm sure thought we were crazy, 'Would you like three of these chairs, we can't do with nine we can only use six.' When we told her that they were £1 a piece she jumped at the bargain, so that was a very good deal for us, and Harold Brown and I formed a firm friendship over the years. He had one tremendous asset, as well as being a great judge of furniture he was as straight as a gun barrel and I was very sad when he died.

Dealers, in those days, seemed to be great characters, and one of them was Ben Nyman. I did all sorts of things with him, and for him. He used to be much more of a porcelain man than a furniture man, in fact, he was known as the 'King of Solon'. Collectors and dealers will know that a very clever Frenchman, Marc Louis Solon, was to bring many financial problems to the Minton factory in the nineteenth century. He came over from the great Sèvres factory in France with his wonderful invention of a sort of ceramic paste, called *pâte-sur-pâte* that was highly expensive. Ben Nyman became fascinated by Solon's work and, of course, those who know what *pâte-sur-pâte* looks like can appreciate this. Practically every bit of Solon's work that turned up in England went to Ben Nyman in those early days. He had a tremendous stock of Solon and he invited me to his house one day and we had a very nice meal together with his wife and my wife. Then we went down into the cellar and, my word, a large old beer cellar under his house was stacked with nothing but *pâte-sur-pâte*, all manner of lovely things. One day I said to him, 'Ben, you know, you must have had a bit of luck when you started.' 'How do you mean?' he said, 'What do you mean?' 'Look,' I said, 'how can you go about the country giving £200 for this and £300 for that. Every day we see your name in *The*

25

Telegraph – pair of Solon vases £600 (Ben Nyman). What do you use for money?' Then he told me this story.

'Well,' he said, 'perhaps I did have a bit of luck. When my father died just before the 1914 war we were absolutely as poor as churchmice, we hadn't a clue where the next penny was coming from and my mother and I really had nothing. We had got the word "China" printed over the door of the shop and we had some toilet-ware in it and that was about all. One day a man came into the shop and asked if I bought china. "If you'd like to go down to the docks and see a chap named Harry," he said, "there is a German ship just put in and left five crates of eggcups on the wharf. I don't know whether they've been dumped but there they are and you'll be able to buy them cheap off Harry." So down to the docks I went and for 30 shillings a time bought five of the largest crates of eggcups one could imagine. Eventually I was so sickened by these things, and I think everybody in the East End must have had some of my eggcups at a penny each or two a penny. The last crate I managed to sell over the phone to another dealer on his condition that they were unpacked for him. Curiously enough, out of this very last crate came not only egg cups but a dozen pairs of Meissen figures! I was so taken aback with these that I straightaway returned to the shop and immediately swept out all the eggcups and every-thing else. I put eleven pairs of figures all along the little window board at £3 and £4 a pair. One pair I've got to this very day and I wouldn't part with them for anything. Those eleven pairs sold in less than twelve hours and next day, with all that money that had fallen out of the blue, I went to Christie's and I bought a little pair of vases for £3. Then I went to Sotheby's and bought a pair for £4, and back again to Christie's and so on. So perhaps I did have a bit of luck!'

Another story he told me was when he was phoned by an

agent for Paul Mellon, the great American collector, who said that Mr Paul Mellon had heard that Mr Nyman had some very fine Solon plates and would he be prepared to sell them. 'Yes,' he said, 'I've got some plates to sell', and took this agent of Paul Mellon down to his cellar and produced about eighteen lovely *pâte-sur-pâte* plates, but the agent said, 'Mr Mellon only wants twelve', 'I don't mind,' said Ben, 'he can have twelve'. On being asked how much they were Ben Nyman quoted '£100 each.' It was a price the agent thought was quite acceptable. Then Ben asked what Mr Mellon was going to do with them. 'Oh,' said the agent, 'he's going to put them on his dining table for his guests to use for dessert.' 'Put them back please,' said Ben, 'I'm not having anybody cut about with a knife and fork on those Solon plates. Put them back again they're not for sale.' That's a simple sort of story, but I'm sure such thoughts often go through many dealers minds. They get so attached to the things they hold dear, and in Ben's case the thought of someone scratching across those Solon plates with fruit knives didn't please him at all.

We had a sale, I suppose twenty years ago or more, a four-day sale down in Wales, and to my astonishment Ben Nyman walked in and shook hands with me. I said, 'What are you doing here Ben?' 'Well,' he said, 'London is so hot and sticky, I knew you'd be down here, where are you staying?' I told him the name of the hotel and he said that he would go and arrange to stay there as well. Later on the sale was well under way and Ben Nyman was buying a number of lots for quite serious money, all manner of objets d'art, carved ivory figures, fine porcelain, and things he particularly liked. I think it is true to say that he wasn't such a great furniture man but he liked anything that was attractive, it didn't matter if it was in metal or porcelain. He came to me during the course of the sale and asked me to look after things for him while he slipped out for a bit. 'You know,' he said, 'anything you think I might fancy.' Well, during the time he was away a bookcase came up, of course these prices are so different now, but this bookcase seemed to be hanging fire at about £40 or £50, so I bought it for about £68 and told the clerk of the sale to put down the purchaser's name as Nyman. About an hour later Ben came back again and said, 'Oh dear, I missed that bookcase, I could have done with that, how much did it make?' '£68', I told him. 'I would have liked that', he said. I suggested he might go and find out who had bought it, for the sale clerk would certainly tell him. He went to the clerk and found that I'd booked it to him, and so that was just another little episode in our friendship.

A funny thing then happened, because the various ivory figures he was buying were German and large and were making £60, £80 and £100 a pair, and the china was also selling very well. So he said to me at the end of the first or second day's sale that he was thinking of taking away the smaller things for safety. I said, 'Yes', of course, but, as he had no cases or packing material, they were put rather haphazardly in his car. I remember this particularly, for he just wrapped them up in newspaper and took them out to his car and went backwards and forwards until he'd got the whole lot in. The car had one of those roofs that used to pull up with no side curtains or anything like that. He was a bit of a fresh-air fiend, was Ben. He always got up early in the morning and had a walk or a bathe, he was a great swimmer, and he drove a very sporty car, a big tourer. At dinner that night, I asked him if he had collected his purchases all right. 'Yes,' he said, 'they're in the car.' All the next day the car stood outside the hotel, with no real protection at all with those precious things wrapped up in bits of paper, under an old sheet. I thought of the way we had carefully nursed those things, taken such good care of them over the weeks we were preparing the sale and during the view days when we hardly let anyone touch them. To think that £3,000 or £4,000 lay out in the street like that, well that was Ben Nyman. 'They'll be all right', he said, and, of course, they were. I think things might be a bit different today.

I suppose those pieces which he bought for £60, £80 or £100, would probably be worth £300 or £400 today, and the large German ivory tankards with plated covers, carved all over with lions and tigers, would be worth £500 or £600 each. When Ben Nyman started bidding and really got his teeth into something, he just walked about the sale and kept twiddling his thumbs, or winking at the auctioneer, doing all sorts of things, and generally managing to get most of the items he wanted. He had a shop in Camden High Street, which I never went to and he had a son who, I believe, still carries on the business.

Of course, when I had my car I was able to get to better types of sales. Now I could go thirty or forty miles to a sale in Oxford or Witney, or somewhere where there would be a representative of the best London dealers. There was a particularly nice young fellow who used to regularly turn up, a George Harris. I hadn't a clue who he was until I discovered he was the son of Moss Harris. The firm of Moss Harris is still about in Tottenham Court Road, very fine dealers in good antique furniture. I used to look at that man and think, 'My, wouldn't it be lovely being George Harris. Fancy being able to come here and be able to give £600 for that bureau bookcase.' The same with the buyer for Rochelle-Thomas. They were a firm known all over the world as possessing the finest dinner and dessert services you could get, they used to buy them everywhere and I recall the buyer's name, Axford, a great judge of porcelain. I should say he had very bad eyesight because he always wore very thick pebble spectacles. He would arrive at a sale in a taxi, and out would tumble about three suitcases, and one knew full well what would go in them. Axford always went for the best porcelains, and I knew there was no earthly chance of being able to buy against him because they were obviously the leading buyers for those things.

Don't imagine that every dealer in England who buys fine goods never makes a mistake. Do not think for one second that they've never had a gamble on a piece of furniture which is obviously genuine and unusual. It is this feature of being unusual that is so difficult to put a value on, and this I found to my cost in more ways than one; and also to my profit in more ways than one. Some special little feature, or some peculiar design, and you find yourself thinking, 'I've never seen an article like that, what on earth is it worth?' In the end, because you like it so well you buy it for about £55 instead of the £30 you first thought of, and you try and get a tenner profit or you might lose a tenner. This is what you call a gamble, but if you love nice things it's nice to handle them and even if I lost a tenner I learned a lot. Somebody might come in and say, 'Well, of course, that's perfectly genuine but these things are so unsaleable you'll never sell it', and so you go on. It is when a good dealer or a good collector talks to you, that is when they give you their knowledge, and for absolutely nothing. If only you can get in the confidence of a good dealer, when he just talks to you and says, 'No you mustn't buy that bit of Derby, because this is Crown Derby, this is so much later than the Derby that we want you to collect' – knowledge oozes out of these men – cultivate their friendship and you get on a lot better.

When I had my shop in Reading, I used to go to as many auctions as I could. Fifty years ago professional expertise in preparing a catalogue was not always used, particularly in country or village sales. The obvious thing was to try and view every sale whether a catalogue stated that objects were antique or not. In those early days I bought anything on which I felt I could get a profit.

At about this time I attended an auction near Slough, and while the early lots were being sold a dealer, who I recognised as being one of the 'big' dealers, came to me and asked if I would join him in purchasing one of the lots. He said it would make a lot of money so I told him that I would be pleased to be part of it. In fact, I was delighted to be associated with such a big dealer. Then I walked all around the large house where the sale was being held to see if I could find anything which I thought might make a lot of money. I could see nothing at all.

After a while the dealer came back to me to say that he had managed to persuade six others to join us. In due course he bid for, and bought for 200 guineas, a marble bust of a man. Being well able to divide by seven, I wrote out my cheque for £30 and took it to him. Then he surprised me by asking if I would mind clearing the bust and taking it back to my shop in Reading. He said that he would call and collect it in due course. So, I was left with the difficult job of getting this heavy marble bust back to my shop.

My wife wondered where we were going to put the valuable bust and, in the end, we decided the safest place would be on the bed in our spare room. So there it lay for the next six weeks, just glaring at us each time we peered at it round the door.

The big dealer then called to see me and suggested, that as I was a young man, and as he had not been able to sell the bust, he would offer me my money back. I refused, not because I had any faith in making a profit out of the bust, but simply because this was the first time the big dealer had given me the chance to join him in one of his deals.

I discovered later that he had visited all the other dealers who had joined him in the scheme, and that he had in fact given back the original shares to four of them. There now remained just three of us, myself, an older dealer, and the big dealer. It was not long before he returned to my shop. 'I've sold it,' he said, 'and it shows you a fiver profit,' and he gave me the cash. I imagined that to be the end of the story but it certainly was not. Meeting the older dealer some months later he told me he had been given £15 profit. It proved to be a bust of William Penn, and it now resides in the United States of America. So it is that you live and learn.

Chapter Three
The Arm of the Law

YOU MAY REMEMBER that I said I was a choir boy at St Mary's
Church and, my word, a very pretty girl used to attend some
of those services. I had a job to take my eyes off her, and it
wasn't too long before I eventually plucked up courage and
spoke to her, a friendship developed and we eventually married. We possibly would not have married so early as we did
except for the following circumstances. My father had died,
as you will recall, when I was seventeen although coming
eighteen. My mother had bought me the little Morris car
when I was twenty-one and we three used to drive about
together, my mother, my friend and me. We had an accident
one day in Reading which turned the car over, and for about
a year my mother lay in hospital and eventually died from
her injuries. The accident caused us to marry when my fian-
cée, Queenie, was only eighteen and so that's why we started
off together so young.

We got married on October 12 1926 and Hilary, our first
daughter, was born on February 1 1928. We were still living
over the shop with all it's inconveniences. Every time the
shop bell rang my wife had to go down two flight of stairs,
then two flights to the baby upstairs. We were very happy
then; I am not going to suggest that we would have gone in
for the 'Dunmowflitch', but we managed somehow or other.

We were no different from other young married couples and this marriage of ours has now gone on for fifty-six years (in October 82). I don't know how other people feel, but there can't be all that many of us today who can boast of fifty-six years together.

Young Hilary went to school in Reading and eventually became a student nurse at St Bartholomew's hospital, London. She passed her various examinations and stayed long enough to become Ward Sister, and then a Theatre Sister. Although I say it myself, she was undoubtedly a very good nurse. When she worked nights, as all nurses would do, I think she worked ten nights in succession and would then come home for four days. All the while she was home she really talked of nothing else but the fact that she ought to be getting back because some poor soul was so ill, or some such thing or the other. In 1932 our second daughter, Anne, was born. She, in turn, followed her sister to St Bartholomew's Hospital and became a nurse.

I expect most parents have had scares which have frightened them over their children. We certainly had one, if not more, but we certainly had one involving Anne. That was when one day I was working in a house at Farnham in Surrey, some thirty to thirty-five miles from Reading. I was trying to value the contents of a house when the phone rang, and I don't know why it was but I felt so strange about hearing that phone bell ring. I thought, somehow or the other, 'I bet that's for me', and it was. When I answered the phone a voice just asked me who I was and then said, 'I have to tell you that your daughter has just been taken to the Babies Nursing Home in Reading, and I would suggest you get back as quickly as you can.' So there we were, and I was in Farnham. I'd gone there by train, and the owner of the house said to me, 'Have you had bad news', and I said 'Terrible, it's my daughter she is only two years old and she has been whipped off into a Nursing Home.' 'Oh dear, oh dear', he said, 'how are you going to get back?' 'Well, I came by train,' I said, 'I don't know how they run.' 'Oh' he said, 'don't be bothered by that, I'll get my car and I'll run you back.' What a great chap he was, we ran out to his car and then he drove me back all those miles to Reading right up to the Nursing Home, where I found Queenie walking about on the pavement outside. They wouldn't let her in because they didn't want the baby to see her mother, and so we walked about outside, up and down, what on earth we thought we were doing I've no idea but we felt we were near her I suppose. Eventually we saw the matron again and she told us that everything was going on fine. Because they did not want Anne to see us we had to creep into a room where we peeped through a screen, and there she was. She was lying in a cot that was half out in the cold air, I looked at my wife and she looked at me, and we wondered what on earth really was going on, but she recovered thank goodness. The matron told us that the child had not suffered pneumonia at all, it was simply that she had never breathed really fresh air before. Where we lived in Reading, right in the middle of the town, there was a narrow street by the side of our shop which was used as a back entrance to a large firm. With the windows open all day long she had been continuously inhaling exhaust fumes from the street. The one thing the matron thought had saved our child's life was the fact that they had pushed her outside, well wrapped up of course, where she had the chance to breathe some really pure air. That wasn't a very pleasant time for us at all.

It was an extraordinary thing, I don't know whether other families have experienced this, but all the usual childish ailments these two daughters had my wife had with them again.

When they had measles, she had measles. When they had scarlet fever, she had scarlet fever. A most odd thing to happen really, because measles, as everyone knows, with an older person is much more serious than when you have it as a child. But she had had it as a child and she also had it again, in fact she had almost everything that the children have had all through their lives.

Soon after I had taken on the shop in Reading I started collecting silver in a modest sort of way, and my great interest then was caddy spoons, because I could afford to buy those Georgian and Victorian caddy spoons for £1 each. £2 would have been a big price to have given for a caddy spoon thirty years ago, and I formed a collection of perhaps two hundred or so, but I sold them after some years because it was practically impossible to display them. I liked them, you could see when Queen Victoria came on the throne by the way the designs differed from the Georgian ones. I tried all ways to show them; if they lay in specimen tables they looked as though the specimen tables were completely empty. But they were interesting, and years ago you could collect things even though you hadn't much money. Every caddy spoon I had was completely different in shape, design, and date, and I had one or two that I particularly liked, those fashioned as tea leaves, lovely little silver leaf shapes with a little tendril handle all synonymous with tea, but as I say, they have all been sold. It would cost quite a lot of money to form such a collection today.

Another favourite relaxation for me at that time was sport, I've been interested in sport for as long as I can remember. Living in Reading over the shop it wasn't too far removed for us to go to Wimbledon, or to any of the Cup Finals at Wembley. Soon after we were married we started going to Wimbledon, and we used to leave Reading about six or seven in the morning and form part of the crowd of people queuing for centre stand seats that were 8 shillings each then. This queue as a general rule got longer, and longer, but, as I say, we'd leave home early and we always managed to get in and have two centre stand seats at 8 shillings each, and sixpence each for a cushion!

Once more I refer to our little Morris Cowley that had one of those canvas pull up roofs. It was on a very showery and wet day when we left Wimbledon at about six or seven in the evening. Actually it was pouring in torrents, and as I adjusted this hood so it split from side to side. Well, Queenie had put on a nice navy blue suit to go to Wimbledon and there we were in this car with no protection at all with the rain absolutely coming down in straight lines. I just wonder what people thought of those two youngsters in that car, driving along in a large concourse of Rolls-Royce and Daimler cars, and us sitting in our car in such pouring rain. Of course we were not long married so possibly they imagined we did not realise it was raining. There is a sequel to it all insofar as I thought to protect my wife, for in the boot of the Morris Cowley was some carpet underfelt that I carried to wrap up any pieces of furniture I might buy. I got this underfelt out and wrapped it around her and, my God, when we got home to Reading the fluff from it, that lovely navy blue suit was sodden, really one of the wonders of the world. Oh dear, it took days and days to clean it and get rid of all the fluff. That is one thing that we really do remember about going to watch tennis at Wimbledon.

We muddled on with our little antique business and then I formed a friendship with another dealer who owned the Reading Fine Art Galleries. He used to come in to me each morning and say 'Have you got anything for me today?' and I'd reply 'No, not this morning, I didn't get anything at the sale yesterday.' Sure enough he'd come back the following morning and I'd say, 'I've just bought this table and chair', and he would buy everything I had bought. Then one day he said to my wife and I, 'This is absolutely crazy what we are doing, you don't want this shop, you don't want to pay the rent and rates on these premises because I buy everything you bring back.' 'Yes you do', I said, because he invariably did. 'Then why don't you do the self same thing and be employed by me?' he said. 'Oh,' I said, 'I don't know that I want to be employed by anybody.' 'I knew you'd say that', he said, but eventually I did go to work for him and I was paid £4 a week which I understood was a very good wage, and all I had to do was to go about England in pursuit of antiques. I could go anywhere I wanted, buy anything I liked and send it back to him, write the cheques and they would all be met, and so that's when I think I really began to get into the trade properly. If someone asked me £30 or £300 for a piece of furniture I could now buy it because the cost would be paid at once into my bank. Consequently, everywhere I went I bought goods. There was plenty about in those days and the prices were so different from what they are now, but the cheques were all met and I had a very free hand. I used to go into that shop on a Saturday, it was the only time I ever went there, for this £4 a week. This was the period when I think I was really starting to look hard at furniture and, of course, I wasn't using my own money. This man said to me, 'Whenever you go to a sale, it doesn't matter where it is, if you can find out the best dealer in the town go and call on him. I don't mind the money that you spend as long as you buy me things we can sell', meaning, of course, that if I could buy, say a sofa table, perhaps for £90 and he could sell it the next day for £100 this was one of the things he wanted me to do.

I revelled in all this freedom, going from sale to sale and shop to shop. The drawback to it all was that I was away from home so much, often for weeks at a time. Even so, I tried hard to be home for any events that involved our daughters. Proud parents the world over know that they possess the cleverest children that there are; we sent our two little girls for elocution lessons, and you can imagine how proud we were when the childrens concerts came along and the girls had to say their pieces. We were always there, of course, and Hilary my eldest daughter, standing in front of fifty or sixty parents would say her piece as right as rain, but Anne, my younger daughter, could only be persuaded to say anything before this crowd of people if she stood under a table. The reason for this, she seemed to think, was that she would be completely unseen if she could stand under a dining table, she wasn't very tall, and so she managed to say her little piece like that, yet she was, of course, in full view of every member of the audience.

Often I was faced with a tug-of-war as to whether I ought to go to a seven- or eight-year-old daughter's concert and miss, perhaps, the opportunity of earning a few pounds at a sale. These are difficulties that always seem to arise if you haven't had a great deal of money. In spite of such problems they were happy days and, what's more, I knew that I was gaining in knowledge and acquiring a certain expertise in antique furniture with every week that went by.

Of course, when the war came along in 1939 it affected the lives of everyone in one way or another. I began to see my days as an antique dealer suddenly coming to an end. Although I was a bit too old to go into the armed forces, prior to the war I had become very much involved in the ARP as it was called, and when the war broke out I was a Deputy Chief Warden. My main task was that on every 'yellow warning' that is the early warning that came prior to the public warning, I had to report to the police station as a liaison officer between the warden service and the police. And so began my three or four years as a policeman, for eventually I was seconded into the Police Force from the Warden Section and worked as a clerk in the CID, although I did once make an arrest.

During the war many bicycles were being stolen, and so it was arranged that a detective and I should go and stand out of sight and watch the queues in the Odeon picture palace. Quite early in the evening, about 6 o'clock, he and I were standing in the shadows watching and completely out of sight. In order to get to the Odeon I had ridden my own bicycle down there and put it against a number of other bikes that were lying there as well. Well, we stood there for an hour or two, perhaps three hours, and I really got so that I couldn't really see anybody doing anything at all, when suddenly this detective said, 'Come on someone's got one.' I said, 'Where?' 'Come on', he said, and we ran across the road and he caught hold of this fellow and lo and behold he'd pinched my bike!

It mustn't be imagined that I was ever a policeman in the accepted sense, someone stopping crime or doing this, that or the other. But on another occasion I was asked if I would keep observation, I was sent into an insurance office that was opposite the post office in Reading, and here again, a bicycle had been placed by the main post box and I was supposed to watch this bicycle in case someone took a fancy to it. Sure enough, someone did. I ran out of the insurance office and managed to catch a chap who was already on the bike and was about to pedal off. I just put my hand on his shoulder and said, 'Come on my friend, come with me to the station, this bike is not yours.' Well, there was some little altercation between us, he swore it was his, but of course I knew it wasn't and so I told him that I must arrest him and took him down to the police station. I gave him to the sergeant in charge, together with the bike, and I thought that was the finish of it, but no, I was absolutely staggered when I was told that I must go to court and give evidence against this chap. That bothered me because I couldn't really remember what I had said to him when I stopped him on the bicycle and I was supposed to tell the court exactly what had happened, which I did to the best of my ability. Really, the intricacies inside a police station are really something to behold at times, there is such a formality about it all, quite rightly I suppose because every report that every constable makes passes through the various offices from the sergeant to an inspector, superintendent and to the chief constable. In the end presumably everybody knew that some fellow had attempted to steal a bike from outside the post office. This might seem to be a bit unnecessary, but there is no doubt about the care with which these reports are written by the various police officers concerned, so that everyone knows exactly what's going on.

Some years before I ever entered the police station I was stopped on a Christmas Eve by a policeman, because he said I was obscuring the number plate on my car. I didn't take too kindly to this because on the back of my car on the luggage rack which unfolded, was a perambulator. I said, 'You can see the number plate.' 'No,' he said, 'You can only see it if you lie on your stomach.' He said he'd have to report me, I said, 'All right, then you do what you like.' Some years later that case was brought back to me because every policeman seemed to know that I'd been a bit saucy to a constable. All my life I've been a stickler for detail, I've got to look for it in antiques and I've always been a bit methodical, any inventory that I have made will have no rubbing out of words or one letter stamped over another, if so it would all have to be typed again. The experience of working inside a police station was quite interesting in a peculiar sort of a way, although one couldn't help feeling a bit sorry sometimes for some of the chaps who were wheeled in.

Reading was extraordinarily fortunate during the war, considering the town's proximity to London. However, one Wednesday afternoon, a German raider dropped four bombs while on his way home from London; they were, I believe, the only bombs to fall on the town all through the war.

When the siren sounded I was already in the police station, in fact I was under it, down in the bowels of the earth. So far as the warden service and Arthur Negus was concerned, our plans and organisation for such an eventuality were, in theory, word perfect. We had carried out exercises through many nights, and on paper we could do marvels.

The first bomb that fell hit the police station and wiped out all our systems of communication. I couldn't get a word to anybody, we couldn't even sound the 'all clear'! Everything was controlled from the police station and all of it was out of order. When the dust cleared we found that several people had been killed, some I had known well. There was considerable damage too, apart from the police station. One casualty was the Reading Fine Art Galleries. The owner said to me, 'I don't know how we stand now, at the moment I haven't got a business at all. I'll get compensation, but what will happen after the war I just don't know, if you see a job you fancy, please don't consider me.'

That single air raid and its results certainly gave Queenie and I a lot of food for thought. The warden service then decided to move its controls four miles out of Reading, although I still reported to the police station when the 'yellow warning' was received. It was during one of those 'warning' periods that I decided to do something that was to prove one of the most important actions I have ever taken in my life. To help pass the time while waiting for something to happen I had taken a copy of *Connoisseur* magazine with me, and while scanning through it I saw an advertisement that caused me to read it very carefully. The advert stated that an old-established West of England firm of auctioneers required a cataloguer, and for reply it gave a box number. I wondered if by any chance it might be the firm of Bruton Knowles; the reason that particular firm came to my mind was because I had always had respect for them. I had always found their sales to be held in good houses, and the descriptions of items listed in their catalogues were exactly what they were said to be, I enjoyed going to their sales.

One of the problems of being a dealer, particularly at that time, was that you could travel a thousand miles a week looking for antiques in auction sales, and not see one thing that was genuinely old. I once went to the West Country hoping to buy a 2-foot Queen Anne walnut bureau, but when I got to the sale I found it was brand new. When these things happened there was no redress, no chance of having expenses refunded, you just had to get in your car and drive home with a wasted day.

Anyway, I answered the advertisement and, sure enough, I received a letter from Mr Norman Bruton of Bruton Knowles, and an appointment was made for me to go down to them for an interview. Mr Bruton said, 'No doubt you have brought me examples of your work.' I said, 'I've never done this before in my life.' 'Oh dear,' he said, 'well I just don't know'. I asked if he kept all records of sales in his auction books, and I suggested he looked at one from the pre-war days at Wonaston Court, Monmouthshire. I remember that sale because it rained for two days and nights and on the last day of the sale we could not get out of the grounds, the rains had flooded the dip in the mile long drive and it was such a pantomime! Anyway, it was a very good sale, and on looking at the auction book my name was there as being the purchaser of several lots. 'Oh well,' he said, 'I suppose if you could buy these things you would be able to describe them.' I agreed, so he said to me, 'I've got one or two things in my own home that I know about, would you mind coming up there and telling me what they are?' So I went up to his home and it was true, he had one or two very good things which I identified to his satisfaction. Mr Bruton then offered me the position of cataloguer, but I said, 'I'm in the police force in Reading, I cannot come until the war ends.' So the post was held for me until I was released from the police force about one year after the war ended. When I did go I had no regrets, and have never had any, because it still happens the firm goes into so many jolly good homes with fine things to be sold.

One thing I must just say, in the nicest possible way, there would have been no Arthur Negus on television if there had been no Mrs Negus. That is undoubtedly, absolutely true, because without her I would never have left Reading. It was Queenie who encouraged me to leave and go to Gloucester. I would have stayed forever muddling about in Reading, and it really was a muddle because industry was closing in on the town, and families were moving out, the families I wanted to deal with that is, and Queenie had the wisdom to see that we had been getting nowhere fast.

Above. The Huntley & Palmer's factory in King's Road, Reading, in 1903; Arthur still vividly recalls the marvellous smell that pervaded the town when they made ginger nuts.

Right. An aerial view of Reading in the 1930s. Broad Street is to the left, and St Mary's church in the bottom right hand corner with Arthur's Minster Street shop on the junction immediately above it.

Previous page. Arthur with his much-treasured and superb inlaid mahogany sideboard, from the workshop of his cabinet-maker father.

Opposite above. Treasure Trove! These mint-condition silver spoons dating from 1638 were found during building works in a Cirencester jeweller's shop in 1966. Arthur was called in to value them, and to advise the coroner whether they might have been stolen and then concealed, or simply lost. He felt unable to comment with his usual assurance of such a matter. The spoons are now in the Gloucester Museum.

Opposite below. The Old Wilsonians' Football team which won the Reading Temperance League Division III about 1920/21. Arthur Negus stands third from the left, back row. He has always retained a keen interest in all sporting activities.

Below. Arthur the Saxon (centre). In 1920 Reading School took part in a town pageant in which the Vikings attacked while the Saxon townsmen were away hunting!

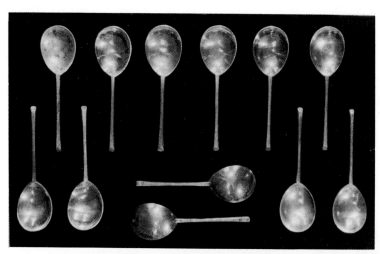

Left. Going for a Song provided viewers with a mass of information about antiques, and made Arthur into a national celebrity. Here he examines a silver candelabrum with Max Robertson.

Below. The Going for a Song studio with Max Robertson in the chair, Arthur Negus and Geoffrey Van as the experts, and Jacqueline Inchbald and Donald Sinden as the contestants. Lindsey Bradshaw, the scorer and

mathematician, is in the foreground.

Right. Max Robertson and Arthur Negus with *Going for a Song* director John King (left) and producer John Irving (right).

Below. Arthur Negus and Bernard Price have broadcast together on Radio 4 in *Talking about Antiques* since 1966. This picture shows an early edition with the programme's first chairman John King.

Above. The *Talking about Antiques* team in the late 1960s, with Mary Lanning, Hugh Scully and Pamela Howe in addition to Arthur Negus and Bernard Price.

Pride of Place with John Betjeman: (*right*) outside Belton House, Lincolnshire and (*far right*) listening to a playback while filming at Syon House in 1966, with His Grace the Duke of Northumberland.

Arthur Negus demonstrating the qualities of a
papier-mâché chair of about 1850. He has
always had an especial fondness for well-designed
and well-made chairs.

Imparting inside information to Robert Holland-
Ford.

Opposite. The Louis XV marquetry table by Jean-François Oeben (*c.* 1720–43) discovered by Arthur Negus in a garage and sold at auction for 34,000 guineas. See page 64.

Right. The piece of furniture that Arthur Negus will never forget. 'Everything about it is remarkable' he says. This magnificent bureau, in the royal collection, was made for Queen Charlotte in 1761. The cabinet maker was William Vile.

Above. An August Bank Holiday trip to a donkey
sanctuary at Ottery St Mary, Devon.

Opposite. Snooker has long been an interest with
Arthur. He modestly claims that he 'could once
play a good club game'. Here, in the series *Negus
Enjoys*, he takes up his cue under the eye of a
world champion, Ray Reardon.

Overleaf. Arthur's dog Hamish.

Chapter Four
Poacher
Turned Gamekeeper

I ABSOLUTELY CHANGED SIDES after forty odd years in Reading trying to buy goods as cheaply as possible, and I have now spent over thirty years in Gloucester trying to ensure that owners receive a fair price for their possessions. It was always a great help knowing so many members of the trade, it was a great help all the way through. I have got great sympathy with the trade, always have had, because all the one hundred and one dealers throughout England who do a fair day's work for a fair day's pay, meaning that they buy goods at fair prices and sell them accordingly, you hear nothing of them. In the same way, there are many excellent firms of auctioneers outside of London who seldom have the results of their sales reported in the salesroom columns of the National Press.

Some of the first catalogues I made for Bruton Knowles, sometimes appear quite funny, because when making a catalogue you walk into a room and find that there's a whole conglomeration of things which have to be given some order. We always sell the china under the heading of 'Porcelain and Pottery', we sell silver under the heading 'Silver', and we sell glass under 'Glass', but you cannot make a catalogue in just that order, so you have to use a book with tear-out pages in order to classify. I remember going into a bedroom once and the first thing I saw was an 8-foot wardrobe, so I thought I can't start with that. You have ideas about how you're going to start. I always start an inventory with the floors, that is the carpets and then the windows, then the curtains, then the fireplaces, then the grates and fenders and then the walls, the mirrors, corner cupboards, anything hanging on a wall, but not the pictures. Having decided I could not start off with that monstrous wardrobe, I decided to deal with things in the order I've described. Then I went round and did the bits of china and any odd bit of silver that might be laying about, and so finished the room. I well remember my astonishment when that catalogue was printed and discovered that in my eagerness not to start with the monster wardrobe I had in fact left it out altogether, so I had to write it in by hand. In those earlier days I always used to go to all the sales where I had made the catalogue, invariably I do now, but I also always went thirty years ago when I was younger. Mr Bruton, who had engaged me, or his son always did the selling, and at this particular sale he said, 'Where has this wardrobe come from?' The porter said, 'It was missed, Sir', and Mr Bruton looked down at me and said, 'I can't imagine anyone not noticing an 8-foot wardrobe!' the audience really enjoyed that. He was a great man was Norman Bruton.

I have always liked auction sales, I like the people. Norman Bruton had such a ready wit, it was as good as going to a theatre to go to one of his sales. If you can imagine how difficult it would be to sell a perambulator, rusty, with no tyres and no hood, an absolutely shocking article, you will realise what an artist he was. When the porter brought it in Mr Bruton said, 'Whatever's that!' 'Lot 62 sir, perambulator.' 'Oh dear,' he said, 'who'll give me one shilling for it?' Of course, no one budged, and he then said, 'if anyone looks at me I shall knock it down to them for a shilling.' Everyone sat with their eyes glued to their catalogues. So then he said, 'I shall knock it down to who I like for one shilling, Lady Gwyn Evans, one shilling, just as well to be prepared Madam.' Lady Gwyn Evans was a charming lady and a great friend of his without doubt, probably about sixty-five at that time, and these were the little asides that used to come so readily from him. People used to love to go to his sales, he was just a natural wit and a very clever auctioneer.

It's all strictly business in the London rooms, but in a nice country house sale, people are all a bit matey and more than a few jokes go by. Of course, when I joined Bruton Knowles in 1946 they had salerooms. The reason that the job became vacant was that the fellow who had been with them before me had died after being with the firm for thirty years. He had run those salerooms for the firm and had got very good salerooms going, but, of course, the curse of all salerooms is the number of iron bedsteads and gas cookers that seem to accummulate, and I did my utmost to get the salerooms shut. Mr Bruton didn't like this at all, but after a few years we did in fact close them down, and as luck would have it, what I thought might happen did. We had all our sales for the next twenty to twenty-five years in private houses. There is no doubt about it, when you have a sale, if the furniture and effects can be sold from their home, the difference in the approach of private people to these things is so much better and so are the prices realised. Salerooms are all right, of course, and I am not talking about Christie's or Sotheby's, I am talking about country auctions in salerooms. A church hall for example where you have, say, a sofa table of some merit standing up against a garden roller, with perhaps five sheets hanging from a hook on the other side of it. In my opinion it's not fair to expect private people to imagine how that piece of furniture might look in their homes. What a difference it is when a prospective buyer is able to walk into a drawing room or a lounge and see that sofa table standing by a window, or seeing a set of chairs set around a nice dining table. For such reasons as that we still conduct a large number of our sales in private houses.

Some many years ago we received instructions to deal with the contents of a mansion just below Monmouth. Those people who live in Wales will, no doubt, well know The Hendrie. The Hendrie was supposed to have, I think I am right in saying, 365 windows in it. That may or may not be a figment of my imagination but it was a lovely mansion and we were instructed to sell off the contents. The letter of instruction that came to us said that the contents were the property of the late Lord Langattock. My story concerns the arrangement of the sale of the magnificent contents. Goodness knows what the sale would bring today, for the auction must have been twenty-five years ago and it lasted for six days. Whilst preparing details for the catalogue I came across a French table. It was standing amidst a stack of furniture in a garage and the sight of that table took me back to the years when I was about twenty-one or twenty-two and the very first house I ever went to in order to make a valuation of the contents. Do bear this in mind, when I was twenty-one or twenty-two, I had gone on for about three or four years in that business of mine in the little shop in Reading and I firmly believed that I knew all there was to know about furniture by that time. A letter came asking me to go and value the contents of someone's home and off I went, not a bit disturbed by the fact that I might see things that I did not understand. At the house I met a dear old lady who said, 'Now you have come to value my things would you mind telling me about one little table?' and I said, 'Of course.' It is a well known fact that anyone with an antique shop will eventually get a letter from someone asking them to value the contents of a home, and the owner might naturally try you out on one piece about which they already had some knowledge. I really don't blame people for doing that. So this lady took me into a little tiny room and pointed to a piece of furniture. 'You're not going to ask me about that table?' I said, 'That's a French table and I don't understand French furniture, I only know about English furniture.' 'Well,' said the lady, 'How do I find out about it?' I told her that I would bring a man who would know and a man I held in very high esteem. Anyone who may read this book and who is as old as I am, will have heard of Charlie Staal, and so it was that he came down to the house and the same procedure happened as before, and at once he remarked what a nice table it was. It was a very small table, the top about 16 inches in diameter, but it was French, and it was Louis XV, and Charlie Staal said, 'That lovely table is worth £2,500. With that, the old lady was perfectly satisfied and left us, I said, 'Look Charlie, I'm supposed to be doing this, but I haven't a clue what the table is.' 'I'll send you details,' he said, which he did. As he was walking away, he stopped suddenly and came back to me, and said, 'Now if ever you should see a French table which you know to be old, and which is mahogany lined, remember this, that such a table was made for the Kings of France, don't you ever forget it.'

Seeing that French table among a stack of broken furniture in the garage at The Hendrie, I immediately thought of that story all those years before. When the table was eventually brought out of the pile for me, I pulled the drawer out and found that it was indeed mahogany lined. I turned the table over and also found that it was beautifully signed. After some research it went to Christie's where it was sold for 34,000 guineas. In addition to selling all the contents of the house, we were further instructed to sell some silver from a bank, and they gave us the authority to go to the bank and take the silver away and arrange the sale of it, which amounted to twenty boxes. Various boxes, locked trunks, plate chests, anything apparently that would house silver had been pressed into use, it was a job full of interest. The silver was grand and in the end we sent the whole lot to Christie's. Unpacking the silver, before we ever called in Christie's, one box looked a bit tatty and taking the lid off the box, I found that it seemed to have got books stored in it. The first book I picked up was soaking wet, apparently the box had been standing somewhere where there had been a constant drip of water, that had perhaps been dripping on it for years. It was absolutely sodden, and as I held the book it just went like a poultice in my hands, no more than rubbish. That book was thrown away, and then I found another book beneath, also sodden. These books didn't disintegrate so that there were pages left lying about, they were just like so much mush, and it was impossible to do anything with them. After two or three books like this, they gradually got drier and the very last book of all was in pristine condition although I must confess it was a book that I knew little about. Here again, we needed advice from Christie's who discovered it was a Book of Hours with illuminations all done on vellum, and I learned a great deal about it. It was eventually found to have twelve full-page illuminations by Van Eyck and Christie's gave it a name, 'The Llangattock Book of Hours' which in due course was sold for £30,000.

Of course, from an auctioneer's point of view, when one is called into a house to sell the contents invariably one needs to bring in an expert in some particular field to advise on certain items. We had a case some years ago whereby we were instructed to sell the contents of a mansion where there was a small oil painting on a panel of The Madonna and Child surrounded by Angels, I forget the size, I should think no larger than 15 inches by 11 inches. Being a painting and obviously of considerable age, it was necessary that we called in an expert to advise on its correct attribution. I'm referring to the well-known Duccio case. Duccio was an Italian master of the late thirteenth century. The painting was attributed to the Duccio School and, as we had no reason to doubt the attribution, this picture was sold as a painting of the Duccio School and realised about £4,000. An export licence for it was then refused.

Now these are difficulties which arise with auctioneers who try to prepare correct catalogues. There was a sale in the country recently that was held by a firm of London auctioneers where a similar error was made, and it is a bit soul destroying when a firm goes to all this trouble, and many firms do, to create or publish an absolutely correct catalogue, and then they find that there has been a slip up by one of the experts who helped to prepare the catalogue. There is nothing more to say about the Duccio, the best thing that one can say about the painting is that it is now in the National Gallery, London, and is catalogued as a genuine Duccio.

Of course, on the other hand, you get results of sales which are extremely good. One occasion which I remember is when we were instructed to sell the contents of a small house with the owner anticipating getting about £4,000 for the entire contents. After the sale, and after all the expenses and commission were deducted, he received a cheque from us for around £8,000 or £9,000. The only thing he could say about that, bearing in mind that he had got just about double that he expected to get, was why on earth did we sell his father's dining table. He said he was offered £20 for it two years earlier and we had sold it for £18! Now, you get people who at times lose all sense of proportion. I don't think that chap was satisfied with that sale, although he got twice as much as he expected; all because of this offer of £20 for his father's dining table which he said we gave away for £18.

I have had one or two reasonable finds up to now, but of course you never give up hope that perhaps one day there will be another astonishing piece of furniture, or that some other surprise will turn up. I think that uncertainty keeps all auctioneers, dealers and collectors on their toes. I know full well that whenever I go into a house and step into the hall, and there's nothing to be seen there worth anything at all, and then I go into a little sitting room on the right where it is much the same, I never can wait to get in the next room. You never know if some lovely bit of furniture or silver, or something of the kind will suddenly turn up and really get you excited, and this does happen. I've had roomfuls of things on the ground floor of a house with nothing really of value or interest among them, and then, upstairs by the side of an iron bedstead may be one of the prettiest little carved Chippendale tripod tables that one could ever wish to see. You never know, you can never tell what may be in the attic. One day I found half-a-dozen Chippendale chairs in needlework upholstery in an attic probably put up there because the needlework was dirty and a bit old. The family had no wish to sell them, so they were just poked up there in a sort of storeroom. There they must have stayed for eighty or ninety years, virtually forgotten by succeeding members of the family until a death came, and then, down they were brought, to fetch £1,000 some thirty or forty years ago, treasure in the attic as people so often like to say.

Of course, I really have a wonderful life, going into so many houses and enjoying the vast possessions that people have in their homes, and I am often asked whether or not I covet any of it. The answer is I do not covet any of it, I can admire it all greatly and I get a tremendous lot of pleasure from it all. Things happen like this: perhaps there has been a death in a family and I have been called in to sell by auction pretty well all the contents of a nice house. I usually take it upon myself to go there and make a catalogue, and for the six weeks or two months that pass between the first time I go to the house and the actual sale, all those things are mine. I get to know them all pretty well by Christian names. I even think to myself, what a lovely bookcase, I'll bet that will be bought by so and so, and invariably I happen to be right, because I know the pieces of furniture that certain dealers like to concentrate on. It is a lovely feeling, I don't want to take them home so I don't really covet them. I'm not envious of the people who own them but I do feel, at least for a month or more that all these things are mine and so nothing is sold at a sale that I've not handled, seen and enjoyed.

Following on from this idea, every so often something turns up in a person's home that brings a lot of money and we think to ourselves 'How on earth did that ever get in that house?' We are rather apt to think that perhaps the former owner went out at night visiting homes without invitation. On one occasion this was disproved to me in no uncertain manner. I was valuing the contents of a home and was listing the contents of a strong room, but there was too much silver there for me to finish in a day. You will realise that one must always know where one has got to when preparing an inventory. Having started on a shelf, say the top shelf, you then start on the next, until sooner or later the time comes to go home, and you leave a gap among the pieces so that you will know exactly where you have got to when you return next day. When I went back the second day it was obvious to me that someone had been in the strong room since I had left it. I went straight to the owner and said, 'Someone's been in your strong room.' 'Not at all,' he said, 'I know they have,' I continued, 'because there is a tiny silver bowl missing.' He said, 'What have I done?' I said, 'I don't know.' 'Well,' he said, 'after you had gone, someone called on me from the local flower show and said they wanted a small prize, and could I give them one, and I said, "Yes of course I can." I nipped down to the strong room and I saw that tiny bowl and', he said, 'I gave them that.' So there is an interesting point, because someone in that village, perhaps for growing the largest marrow or the best carnation or onion, now has a George' I covered silver sugar bowl worth a few hundred pounds. Perhaps in another hundred years time it might come on the market and the same thought might go through someone's head: how on earth did this little silver bowl get in the possession of that person!

It's quite surprising too how you can, in ignorance, cause some consternation. For example, I was talking in an interview on television to Lord Montague of Beaulieu, and I found him a very nice pleasant gentleman, so easy to talk to and so interesting to listen to. As time went on I eventually said to him, 'I think my Lord we shall have to move on now, we should go into the museum and see some of your "old crocks" ', at which he became quite indignant and said, 'Mr Negus not old crocks I beg of you, all my cars are veterans.'

I don't know which I prefer most of the two things I particularly like doing. One is the pleasure of being with fine things on television, and the other is being with lovely objects in someone's home. They are so closely knit together that there is no choice between the two for me, because in either instance one usually is required to identify articles. On television, in *Going for a Song* or *The Antiques Road Show* an owner may bring along something wonderful and he or she has to be told what it is. The same thing happens in a house, for example, you go into a dining room where there may stand a fine dining table and people who buy our catalogues will need to have it described to them. On the one hand I might well be isolated in a house for two days preparing a catalogue, on the other I might be surrounded by a few hundred people in a hall and facing a camera. Yet basically the same thing always goes over in my mind: what is that article? On TV you openly tell the owner that you think he has a fine piece of Chippendale furniture and usually you receive their approval and thanks. When you print what you think in a catalogue the only time you receive any comment from anybody at all is if you happen to have described it incorrectly.

When I first joined my firm after the war, there were just two of us in the Auction Department, my secretary and myself. It was a good business then, and I like to think it is a good business now, so far as the firm is concerned. The only difference now is that there are seven of us in this small department. During those years I've been with the firm I've had youngsters around me, and through my hands, who have now turned themselves into very good assistants. There is one particular instance I like to recall in this respect. An auctioneer in the West Country sent a letter to the firm asking if they would take on his daughter as a secretary, and could she be secretary to Arthur Negus. He wanted her to return to his business in order to catalogue goods that came into his auctions. The man was told that we could not especially place a girl with any particular person on the firm but the first thing that would be necessary, would be for her to learn shorthand and typewriting. Back came a letter to say that he had sent his daughter to a shorthand/typewriting school, and when she was proficient he would write to us again, which he did.

So this girl was engaged by us as a secretary, and she did eventually become my secretary. She proved to be a most extraordinary girl in that she wanted to learn about furniture, and she wanted to sit the examinations of The Auctioneers Institute. Many, many times, there have been quarrels between us, not nasty quarrels, but I would ask her questions and she would give me all the wrong answers, and I then would get a bit exasperated with her. About two years later she took her exam, and she was the only girl sitting this examination in London, with about thirty other fellows. She brought back the exam papers that she had been given to the office. These papers purported to be a letter from a firm of solicitors asking her to go to a certain room in a museum in London. Their client had left the entire contents of the room at his death and it all needed to be described and valued for probate. Now this was the sort of thing that she and I had been doing during those earlier years, and it proved not too difficult for her. The examiners were so enamoured with her replies and the paper she put in that they struck a gold medal especially for her. The story has a particularly happy ending because, although she didn't return to her father, she married one of the other employees in our firm and they now run a very successful estate-office business in Berkshire.

It's a funny thing how you can get into the habit of describing things in a certain way, and it was something I had not realised. One day, while in London, a man came up to me and asked whether I'd been instructing anybody in antiques lately. I said I hadn't. 'We've just had a batch of papers come in for me to mark', he said (he was the examiner for the examination I've just mentioned). 'I haven't got a clue who the papers belong to,' he went on, 'they are only numbers to me and I don't know who they are at all, but one man has absolutely answered every question in your language. It's all just as though you've sat down and written the answers to every question.' Of course it transpired that this paper was sent in by another of the young assistants of mine. I suppose he had it all so dinned into him by me. That this was so and so, and don't forget to mention these cabriole legs and that bit of carving, look at the brackets, and so on, all this he had written down so that an examiner identified the answers as being written in Arthur Negus language. Anyway, that fellow passed, so perhaps that wasn't so bad after all.

I must confess I haven't got many hobbies, but you see, where one's work is really one's hobby there is no trouble at all. I once had a bit of a skin infection, nothing very much, only that my head got a bit larger than it is today. The skin specialist who came to see me discovered that I had suddenly become allergic to gold and silver. He then said to my wife, 'What does he do on a holiday, what does he do when he goes away?' Of course, she replied, 'Oh, he goes to all the decent houses he can find, or museums.' The Doctor turned to me and said, 'You are absolutely ideal for a skin-infection, you never stop do you, you're absolutely ideal.' It is true I do find visiting homes and museums so pleasant and so enjoyable that I'd much rather be walking round a dusty museum than going in a punt down the river. You know, it is rather funny to talk about myself in this way, but my interest lies in these things, and as I've said so many times there is always the chance that something is going to turn up, and the feeling that you are going to find something which is wonderful. So I shall hope to go on even a bit longer, I have no idea how it will all end but at the moment everything seems to be going along very nicely. One thing that certainly pleases me is that I have given a number of talks all over Britain and what pleases me more than anything else is seeing a couple of thirty-year-olds who are interested in the subject I am talking about. It does seem to me, as much as I enjoy meeting everyone, that it's not all that good talking to people of my own age. I am so pleased to learn there is a younger element who are interested and who will carry on this interest, loving the whole business of enjoying and living with antiques, and that gives me great confidence for the future. I believe there will always be a great number of people who will be interested in fine articles, and the pleasure I have had out of them is immense. I really do consider myself a most fortunate man to have spent most of my life among nice things.

Chapter Five
Antiques–
Knockers and Reflections

I WAS ONCE ACQUAINTED with the keeper of gold and silver at Buckingham Palace. He asked me if I would like to go and see the collection and of course I jumped at the idea and soon it was all arranged. My wife and I felt so grand when we drove through those great iron gates down to the side of the Palace to ring a bell at the side door. I did just that, and the door opened and I said, 'I have an appointment to see the keeper of the gold and silver.' 'Oh yes, Mr Negus,' said the man who answered the door, 'would you park your car just over there and I will go and fetch him, he'll be here by the time you get back.'

Sure enough that's just how it happened. So we were escorted up and into a room, a large gallery one might say, with glazed cabinets all round the walls. This was during the reign of King George VI, and Queen Elizabeth. We were conducted into a fine room and the fellow started undoing all the doors and asking me what I would like to see first, I said that I would really like to see the Gold Service. He took out a plate and gave it to me and I turned it over and had a look at it and I said, 'Silver gilt, George III about 1767', 'Yes,' he said, 'what did you think they were?' 'Well,' I said 'I thought the gold service would be gold.' 'Oh no,' he said, 'no, no, it's a silver gilt service and you can cut on the plates as much as you like but you won't show up any silver.' So that was the first thing I saw, and then he opened up all the cabinets and said, 'You can touch and bring out anything you want, do anything you like with any of it, for it all has to come out to be cleaned in time for a Banquet where we always make a display. He explained to me how Her Majesty allowed him to make the display in the Banqueting Hall and how Her Majesty always came down and saw it just before any of the other guests were due to arrive. He told me how she was always so gracious, and said, 'Oh how so very nice, again thank you very much.'

We had a wonderful day there because, as I say, every cupboard was open and I was amazed to see that all the members of the Royal Family had little collections of their own. The first large cupboard was labelled 'The Nation's Silver' and there were some glorious pieces of silver in that. Then came 'His Majesty's Silver', 'Her Majesty's Silver', 'Princess Elizabeth's Silver', 'Princess Margaret's Silver' and then 'Her Majesty Queen Mary's Silver'. As I went from cabinet to cabinet, it became absolutely obvious to me that here, in point of fact, was a family, a real family. I like to think they were just trying to live an ordinary sort of normal life, because there were little gifts that Her Majesty Queen Mary had given to the two princesses, with little inscriptions on them which said 'From Granny'. It became so apparent that behind all the functions, the uniforms, the pomp and circumstance, here at least was a family just enjoying gifts that a granny would give to her grandchildren, or a mother or a father to their daughters, and I was absolutely fascinated by everything.

Another little thing which showed in that huge and lovely

Palace, was when the keeper came back and said 'How are you getting on?' I said 'Absolutely fine'. He said, 'You can stay as long as you like' and I said 'Well, I've been through everything. Marvellous isn't it?' 'Would you like a drink?' he said. So of course I said that would be grand. He took us along some corridors and then opened a door and closed it behind us, we seemed to be in a little ante-room of some sort, and there stood a chef with a great tall white hat who said, 'What would you wish to drink?' As I stood there looking about the room I noticed that on the door was a photograph of the Arsenal Football team, and there again, I thought; well fancy, in all this huge Palace when you just get away from the main corridors, here was this picture any butler or chef might have put up behind a door anywhere, just a photograph of his favourite football team.

I have always enjoyed looking around great houses, and some years ago my wife and I visited a stately home where we met the owner and his wife. They invited us to have a look at the furniture and, while we were walking through the hall I noticed a very fine pair of chairs. He went marching on in front of me, and this was a real live Duke, an awfully nice man. I said, 'Just one moment sir, I can't go by these chairs. Just look at that chair, what a snorter! Oh, I see you've got a pair.' 'Yes,' he said, 'we've got a pair, forty-eight arms, two settees and four stools at the last count.' I did feel a fool. Going on after dinner that night we were all walking round, the Duke, and the Duchess, and my wife and I. The Duchess and my wife were walking along the long corridor in front of us and the Duke and I were following, when he said to me, 'I've always had great doubts about this table.' It was a gilt gesso table. I said, 'It's impossible to tell whether a gilt table like that is old or a reproduction unless one gets underneath.' 'Well, let's get underneath', he said. So he and I disappeared under this 6-foot wide table to hear someone say, 'Well, where are they? I thought they were following us', and so the Duke popped his head out and said, 'Here we are' and there we were, together under the table. I struck matches to examine the underside of the table and found it to be genuine.

The one thing that I have met all my life has been furniture. Wherever I go, whatever house I go into or whatever sales I attended before I joined my firm, I only went for furniture and, in all houses there is always furniture. There is always a certain smattering of glass, silver, porcelain and pottery and other things, but the one thing you can be certain of is that you are going to see some furniture whether it be good or bad. Although I've been daubed with the word 'expert', this is a word which is often thrust at me, I've never used it myself. All I have ever said is, 'I like furniture.' I think this word 'expert' is an extraordinary word because if one speaks the truth, and I try to, one has never really finished learning. There are so many facets of what we call the Fine Arts that it becomes impossible to know all about everything.

One thing that always amazes me with furniture is that owners apparently do not see the things I see. For example, let's take a chair and there are more chairs about than anything. The first thing I look at is underneath it, because the one thing I feel sure most people have forgotten, is if any particular chair is old, when it started life it was brand new. All it has ever done is to get old, and consequently the application of black stain and hammer marks and excessive wear on it always makes me think that the chair is wrong and invariably it is. When I say to an owner, now look at these marks around the back of the chair here, can you see where that has been hit with the pane of a hammer? 'Yes I can', they say, but they do not always recognise these marks, perhaps it's because they haven't seen so many as I have. Of course, the wood itself is a great giveaway to age, because all through the eighteenth century and part of the nineteenth, wood matured for ten years before it was ever used. It may have been cut and left floating about in log form, before it was cut into planks for drying out. This process took about ten years until the wood became one colour right through. So when I look at the edges on a chair, or the back where there's been some wear, or the front seat rail, or where the legs are bruised, if they show white edges it's because they have been stained to make them look old. Such furniture cannot be old, there is no magic about such things, it is just a matter of using your eyes intelligently.

Years ago, I think the trade engineered a sort of mystique about antiques. They were not so open about it all as they are now. It was then all a bit of a mystery for most people and all knowledge was jealously guarded. A good dealer would say whether a piece was genuinely old or a reproduction but not necessarily say why. Nowadays there's not all that great deal of difference between the price of an ordinary antique and a very good reproduction. I'm not sure what has caused the great interest in antiques that has grown over the last fifteen years. The inflationary period that we have, or are going through, causes people who have money to invest in antiques, feeling it may be better to have something more tangible than ready cash. That may be one reason why there is this interest. Another reason, which has been laid at my door is that I created the interest, with the various BBC programmes on the subject. The programmes I have been associated with may have woken up the latent interest that was already in people, but it certainly did not start it, for the British people have always been collecting.

So many people pretend to be wise after the event when it comes to advice on investing. Strange though it may seem, the best time to have bought antiques was in the early years of the war. On reflection, it seems that I lost all contact with everybody but the police during the war. For some reason I have no recollection of realising that the market in furniture had gone to pot, people were being bombed incessantly in London, pieces of furniture were going through the salesrooms in London, and not only furniture but silver, porcelain and everything else. The prices realised were really quite small but I seem to have no memory of this whatever. I never bought or did anything whatever to try to find out what was happening in the Fine Art market once I got into the police force, that seemed to take everything from my mind. I remember a man coming up to me just about when the war started and he said to me, 'Do you want to make a fortune?' I said, 'Oh well, who doesn't!' 'What you'll need to do', he said, 'is to go and buy a cave in Wales somewhere, and be very choosey about what antiques you buy but take all the things to this cave and forget about them.' 'Then,' he said, 'one of these days when you go in there, you'll find you've made a fortune' and that, of course, was absolutely true. The point about all these investment ideas is this, if you must invest in a gamble like that, it must be with money that you will not want so that you will never be forced to go and sell items in order to replenish your bank account. I had not got that sort of money so could not take up the idea, which would have proved most successful, had I been able to do it.

Of course, there were one or two dealers and collectors who had confidence and pluck to go on buying more or less as they had done prior to the war. Those people who managed to do that, and who managed to survive, came out of it very successfully. One dealer who I knew well, before he went off to the war, simply put all his stock into a storeroom and left. When he returned after the war, and after all those years had gone by, he found he needed to call in another dealer to revalue his stock for him, because things that he'd marked for £7.10s or £6 or £12 were now worth £45, £38, and £80, a remarkable transformation. He often said to me, 'My God! I was thankful to get the help of that dealer, because I had no idea what these things were worth', and of course it's gone on like that ever since.

Over the past six or seven years I've been one person in England who's given a lot of advice to many people and even had the temerity to suggest that the top had been reached in the Fine Art world, only to have it proved completely wrong. I still wonder, surely one day the top must be reached, you cannot go on just buying indiscriminately, knowing that in a year's time you'll be able to show a profit, it really is quite a remarkable situation. It is so terribly difficult to forecast what will happen. I am often asked what might be bought that will be worth more money in a year's time, and I've not the slightest idea. Of course, during 1981 the recession did affect the prices of certain articles to some degree. The interesting part about it all was that the finest pieces of furniture or Fine Art, no matter what they were, the finest pieces sold during the recession made more money. It was the second class goods, the damaged articles, they were the things that showed little or no increase. I asked one or two dealers about this trend and they said, 'We simply don't want to buy anything that's not absolutely top class. Anything out of the top we can sell today quite easily, but anything that's a little bit off, we don't want it at any price.' When you get that attitude from top dealers it reflects right through the trade in no time. So the old adage again seems to be true, that quality must be the criteria of what is bought. I'm afraid that many people who have been, what they like to call investing, in certain commodities in the Fine Art world, may be in for a bit of a surprise when they try and realise on those investments. If they have not been very choosey and bought tip top articles then they may be in quite serious trouble. You see, somehow, some people believe anything that is old is worth money, well of course that's a complete fallacy. Many, many items, are old and virtually unwanted even in this day and age, and it's quite wrong just to go collecting things that are old because they are cheap.

When asked what period of furniture I like best of all, and I must confess that I do have a favourite, although I like all old furniture. I am more attracted perhaps to the work of George Hepplewhite than to anyone else. What first drew me to this man was the fact that nobody knows when he was born, and that's one thing I cannot understand. They know when he died but they don't seem to know when he was born. He was apprenticed to Robert Gillow of that remarkable firm, Gillows of Lancaster. I don't know when Robert Gillow started his workshop there, but I suppose between 1710 or 1720. He married in Lancaster, and Gillows went on and on over the centuries making very fine furniture. Hepplewhite was apprenticed there and he became known, and I think quite justly, as the finest chair-maker there ever was. It fascinates me to remember the very early designs of William Kent, those really heavy pieces of furniture, made only for enormous houses, for some of the finest mansions in the land, particularly Chatsworth, which is almost entirely furnished by William Kent. Then Chippendale comes along and adopts some of his designs but lightens them all, not in colour but in structure. When I talk about this lightness it simply means that instead of the very heavy legs on chairs, Chippendale gracefully took them down a bit, and eventually got rid of the very costly cabriole legs, in favour of square legs. When George Hepplewhite came along, he, as it were, adapted a mass of Chippendale, designs but lightened them still further, so that some of the chairs looked as though it would be impossible for a man to sit in one of them. Hepplewhite took the stretchers away from the legs of chairs. They are so beautifully made that a small Hepplewhite armchair with its beautiful shape and delicate arms on equally delicate moulded cabriole legs with a scroll toe, are to my mind some of the nicest pieces of furniture you could ever look at. He was attracted to French designs, in fact there are certain types of chairs that we call French Hepplewhite. It doesn't mean to say that such chairs were made in France, they were all made here in England to the designs of Louis XV or Louis XVI. Everything to do with Hepplewhite I think is absolutely grand. The lines of his furniture just flow and he was virtually the last to make such attractive furniture before it gradually became heavier and yet heavier again. Thomas Sheraton, on the other hand, wasn't a cabinet maker at all. He wrote a book in which were published all sorts of designs, but when one gets into the nineteenth-century, then to my mind all the gracefulness of eighteenth-century furniture departs with the advent of Victorian furniture. So it's George Hepplewhite for me with everyone else running a very close second.

This leads me to think about the furniture that is being made today, because this does seem to occupy the thoughts of many people. I suppose I may have been a little outspoken at times about my ideas on the furniture that is being made today, and they are pretty well summed up by saying that there is almost none. When I say that, what I really mean is that there is practically no furniture being made today to twentieth-century designs. I'm lucky enough to know one or two cabinet makers with great skills, but these skills are exercised in making very fine copies of Chippendale chairs, or Sheraton sideboards, or fine mirrors, all to eighteenth-century designs. I cannot seem to find anyone who is really making furniture today in quantity to twentieth-century designs. John Makepiece makes fine furniture down in Devon and I found him making really splendid furniture today to twentieth-century designs. What disappointed me so was the fact that with his great skills, and he has great skills, he will only make one piece of furniture to a specific design. I'm concerned that there are many youngsters today who would willingly buy modern furniture made to twentieth-century designs. Furniture as such has been left miles behind, it seems to me, in comparison with other areas of design. I think of silver, and there are some ultra modern designs being carried out in silver by well known silversmiths today that are absolutely twentieth-century if they are anything at all; and people are buying these things, quite naturally. It isn't everybody who wants a George III silver goblet or a George III pair of silver candlesticks, and the same with jewellery. We all know what lovely pieces of modern jewellery there are about, but where are the equals of this jewellery and silver in furniture? That loss is what I deplore.

Having said all this on radio, I was invited to go to London to see a piece of furniture which a man had made, and sure enough I saw a really magnificent knee-hole desk made in coromandel wood, absolutely beautiful, done certainly to twentieth-century designs. I said, 'Did you make that?' and he said, 'Yes,' so I said, 'Well it's exactly what I'm talking about. Do you mind if I ask you what you got for it?' He said, '£9,000.' Now that is not quite what I mean, for I would have thought there was a big market for more ordinary but well-made pieces of twentieth-century furniture at a cost people can afford. Maybe I'm wrong, maybe it needs a lot of money to start off on a project, maybe there are all sorts of things that crop up which deter clever cabinet makers from branching off in this field, but in my view the twentieth-century looks like going down as the one century when no decent furniture was made in quantity. It must not be assumed from a statement like that that I deplore the modern furniture there is. I am not particularly enamoured towards pieces of furniture made of laminated wood, but there are many firms, one in particular I recall, that have popularised elm more than ever anyone thought could be done, and they make some jolly good chairs and tables in elm. There are similar things being made in other parts of the country. In Yorkshire there is a firm making good furniture, but to my mind they all make copies of things that have gone before. If I refer to the elm chairs, they are nearly always stick-backs and wheel-backs. One can get refectory tables, and side tables, all to some degree looking like the old original ones and I would hope that one of these days some of those firms will branch out and make really modern chairs. I know that these trad-itional designs are as popular as ever they were and that pleases me, but I can't help feeling it would be nice to see someone with the ability to make a chair which one would recognise in years to come, and say, 'That chair was made by so and so and it was first produced in 1982.'

Of course one cannot forget the names of one or two firms and individual people who made furniture during the early parts of this century. Heal & Sons, for example, made some very good furniture which today can be recognised. One can walk into any house and say, 'Those two beds are by Heal, that wardrobe is by Heal.' So you can with the furniture of Gordon Russell, and my word they are of lovely quality. Then there are cabinet makers like Gimson, Barnsley & Waals, who made furniture between the wars in the Cotswolds. Here again, I can and I dare say many other people can, walk into a house and say, 'There's a piece of furniture by Barnsley', or 'that must be by Gimson.' Those men did not seem to want to talk to one another, but my word they could certainly make furniture, and they made it to their own designs. When I say I could walk into a house and recognise their work, it's simply because of the design. You'll never be able to say, 'That's a Negus piece of furniture' but there must surely be somebody who could design something that would be recognisable as being made during the 1980s. There can't be much identity in a quantity of chairs and settees that are all made to the same design more or less copying the old ones. Comfort these days is a thing which is in my mind. These enormous divans, or easy chairs at least 6 inches off the ground, certainly one wallows in such things but when one gets to my age it is difficult to get out of them, and if pulled up out of them I usually get a backache. There are far too many costly articles being made today, particularly in upholstered furniture, in which none are different from the other, yet if you think back, there were enormous differences between a Queen Anne settee and a Chippendale settee or a Victorian sofa, nowadays everything seems to have lost its identity.

Having already stated that I enjoy visiting the great houses of Britain and their contents, I also realise that many people might not feel quite like I do. They might even be envious of these homes but there is little doubt in my mind that without them there would not have been many antiques about in this country today. By that I simply mean that the good old days, as they were called, were far from good old days, as I think must be appreciated now by everybody. Some people were very wealthy, the majority of people were poor, no two ways about it. If, say in Queen Anne's time, one landowner could give £25 for a pair of modern candlesticks none of his employees earning perhaps five or six shillings a week could possibly have bought such a pair. The fact that the same pair of candlesticks today might bring £2,500 is immaterial. It should be remembered that it was those people who were the landowners in the eighteenth century, who sponsored Chippendale and his contemporaries and whose homes today contain fine possessions, and I think it is a marvellous thing that such houses are now open to the public. When one visits such houses, seldom does one recognise wealthy people walking around, you see ordinary folk, like myself, and younger people with their children looking around. They do not always know what they are looking at, but they are saying 'Look at that', 'look at that', 'but that's nice.' I love to go and see all the hundreds of people that are wandering about, munching sandwiches, tripping over the drugget which is laid over lovely Aubusson carpets and saying, 'Oh, look at that.' There is little doubt about it that these owners' forebears were the patrons of all the fine cabinet makers. If you look in Chippendale's Directory and see the number of subscribers to the book which was first published in 1754, it is like reading through Debrett's Peerage, but these were the people who were behind the cabinet makers. Chippendale's furniture has lived on, he was called the High Priest of Mahogany, but can you imagine living through the eighteenth century when everybody had a crest, and everybody had their portraits painted over and over again, yet there is no known portrait of this master cabinet maker. Even so the aristocracy recognised the great skills in this man's hands and in the workmen he employed, and they sponsored him.

It could be argued that many up and coming artists are sponsored to some degree by the Arts Council today, but one must have reservations about this. I'm not particularly amused by the amount of bricks that went into the Tate Gallery as a work of art. The aristocracy that lived before were not faced with many of the problems of today. There were not the one hundred-and-one plastic things, and laminated wood furniture, but they recognised talent in men. These four great men, let us name them, Thomas Chippendale, Robert Adam, George Hepplewhite, and Thomas Sheraton.

Way back to the sixteenth century one talked of Elizabethean furniture and one can continue talking about Cromwellian chairs, Charles chairs, William and Mary chairs, Queen Anne furniture, George I mirrors. When these four superb craftsmen were alive, the monarchy was pushed to one side. Then, people talked about a Chippendale chair, an Adam mirror, a Hepplewhite chair, a Sheraton sideboard. Yet, when they had all died, and they had all died by about 1807, what happened, immediately the monarchy was back. Regency furniture, George IV furniture, William IV, and Queen Victoria furniture, all referred to again under name of the monarch.

It's an extraordinary thing how often people are apt to stop me in the street and say, 'I wouldn't like your job.' I say, 'Wouldn't like my job, what does that mean?' Always looking at chairs and tables they reply. I say, 'Yes, always looking at chairs and tables' but then I ask them, 'Do you go to friends houses?' When they say yes I ask if they have ever seen one chair anywhere which looks like the chairs they have. The answer is usually no. So I say that's the whole joy of all these things. People own chairs and tables, but I don't think I have ever seen, in any one house, anything that matched in other houses. There are always the little bits of detail which people miss, extra little pieces of carving on the centre of the splats, the unusual features, such as a carved bird on the splat. The finials on fine shaped arms of Chippendale chairs, perhaps finishing in eagles' heads. The legs, every leg square and chamfered, but some with egg and tongue mouldings down the outside, others with little carved brackets, apparently all looking the same to some people and yet being so different. This is the fascinating part of trying to learn about old furniture, and I concentrate more and more on the study of old furniture. The one-hundred-and-one different things there are on one-hundred-and-one Chippendale chairs is what intrigues me so, these little extra bits of detail.

Covet is not the right word, but nevertheless I would certainly love just one piece of furniture which I saw many years ago at the British Antique Dealers Fair held at Grosvenor House. Everyone will remember how their Majesties always loaned a work of art to that great event, it might be a fine sculpture, or a fine piece of china, it might be silver; but in this particular instance they had lent a mahogany cabinet. That piece of furniture I shall never forget, it is featured in the *Dictionary of English Furniture*, and believe me the grilles above it, and the bombé shape of the drawers underneath, in fact everything about it is remarkable. Perhaps in that one particular instance covet could be the right word. The cabinet is illustrated in the *Shorter Dictionary of English Furniture* by Ralph Edwards, Plate 33 on page 82.

I know a number of people, in fact many people, are very concerned about dealers who go round trying to buy antique furniture at the door. For many years I was a dealer, and whilst I haven't actually been round knocking doors I've certainly been taken to houses by people who have knocked doors. It's not to be assumed for one moment that every person who knocks on any door and says 'Have you any antiques for sale?' is a rogue. You see, the business of antique dealers, and the difficulty for antique dealers, is not so much the buying of things from houses but the getting into houses. This is their biggest problem, how to get in. The unscrupulous people are of course the ones who get talked about so. If any dealer knocks upon any door and the owner has nothing to sell, quite obviously the thing to do is for the owner not to allow him to come in. This is where all the trouble starts. I've had many occasions where clients have rung me up and asked me to go and stop the sale of something which has happened an hour or two before because they have discovered, perhaps after looking at an inventory, or for some other reason, they have found that they have virtually given something away. Now, I go back to these houses, and I say to the owner, 'Now what's happened?' and they say, 'well a man knocked on the door, and I invited him in because he said he wanted to buy jet.' Now that's a very famous way of getting into a house, for most old ladies have jet. I then say, 'Did you give him a cup of tea?' The answer is usually, 'As a matter of fact I did, for he was such a nice fellow.' Then I discover that the owner had then accepted an offer of £50 for a diamond brooch and at the time they were quite happy with that. Later they looked at their inventory and found it had been valued at £350. Immediately they classify the dealer as a rogue, yet the man has done no wrong, and neither has he in my mind. He's politely knocked the door, asked if they have some jet, he doesn't buy the jet but he has offered £50 for something for which the owner has said yes. It is only when these few unscrupulous dealers go about doing this, and manage to get in and make a killing that they get renewed energies to go on doing it. If they moved around England for a month or two and never bought a thing, quite naturally it would all end, because they are in business to buy goods. This is the knocker's method of trying it on and it poses very serious problems. I suppose, people being what they are, some will always allow them into their homes and in some dealers' hands will always be done down. Any sensible person will simply say, 'No, I have nothing I wish to sell, good morning.' Such dealers will go away, and it is very unlikely that they will break in, they abide by the law so far as that goes. The safest plan which has been said so often on television, on radio, in every magazine under the sun, is if you have the slightest doubt about anyone don't let them in, that's the simple answer.

This is the sort of thing that can happen. I was called to a house after the owner had died, and I was there making a catalogue when suddenly the bell rang. I went to the front door and there stood a dealer. He said, 'Can I see the lady?' I said, 'I'm sorry my friend, she is dead. There's nobody in this place but me.' 'Oh,' he said, 'what a pity, I bought one or two things from her the last time I came round.' 'Well,' I said, 'I'm sorry, you're too late now.' 'What are you doing here?' he asked. 'I'm making a catalogue', I replied. He said, 'It's no good me coming in is it, you can't sell anything?' I said, 'No.' So we parted and away he went. I didn't think he had recognised me at all. That night a lady rang me up who lived in that self same village, in fact who lived within twelve houses of the one I had been working in, and she said, 'Did you send a man to my house today to buy furniture?' I told her I had not. 'Well,' she said, 'I had a man call, and he said he was visiting this village with Arthur Negus; Arthur Negus was down the bottom of the hill, having a deal down there, and had I got anything I could show him that would interest Arthur Negus, because he was with him and would be glad to buy it.' Now, this was obviously an unscrupulous dealer who recognised me, and then used the knowledge that I was there as a key to get in to other houses. Whether he got into any homes or not I shall never know, but he certainly did not get into that one, which as a matter of fact was absolutely filled to the front door with fine antiques.

I did once have a disturbing letter come to my home in which a lady stated that she was very surprised that I should send a man to her house who had given her £6 for some books which she had now found to be worth £50. She said, 'I really thought you were more honest than that and wouldn't really do anything like that to anyone.' Of course, it was a complete fabrication, I hadn't sent anybody to any house in my name. The man had gone there, no doubt saying he was buying things for Arthur Negus, and she let him in and he made that killing. I had to write to my solicitors about it all because it was such a serious thing and it had to be stopped. Eventually the man was traced and was given clearly to understand that he must never use my name in those circumstances again, and as far as I am aware he never has. These are the lengths to which one or two of these men will go, so let me stress this again, their difficulty is to get in, and if by using my name, or saying they represent me, the door opens more easily then they will try that too.

Strange things do happen. A newspaper reported recently that I had been helping the police in the recovery of certain sculptures stolen from a church. As a matter of fact, I hadn't got a clue what it all meant because I had not been in touch with the police nor had I been to any church, so I took no notice of this. The next day I received a letter from the Chief Superintendent of the Police thanking me for all that I had done in helping the church recover the sculptures. This clearly needed some attention by me, because I still had no idea what they were talking about. I made an appointment to see the Superintendent. I said, 'I haven't given any help to anyone', so he called in a Detective Inspector and asked, 'What is all this about sculptures stolen from a church? Mr Negus knows nothing about them.' The Detective Inspector said, 'I have a statement where he had said the sculptures are worth £1,000 apiece.' I said, 'I have no idea what you are talking about, no one has interviewed me.' The mystery deepened, but the Chief Superintendent told me he would get to the bottom of it and sure enough he did. This is the silly thing that happened. Apparently, the vicar of this church (and to this day I do not know where it was) had photographs of the two sculptures, and said to one of his parishioners that Arthur Negus ought to see the photographs. He was told by the man he was talking to not to bother to send them to Arthur Negus as he would be seeing him and would let him have a look at them. The photos were returned to the vicar, without my knowledge, and the man who had taken them said, 'Well we think these must be worth about £1,000 each.' It was the vicar who was then interviewed by the constable who, quite sincerely and honestly, said, 'Arthur Negus has seen these and he says they are worth £1,000 apiece.' That's how such stories can get about and become twisted in the process. It all proved to be quite an extraordinary tale because there was not a very pleasant ending to it. Here was I, the innocent party to it all and, about two days after the newspaper report had appeared, we had a very large stone thrown through our windows in Cheltenham. Some people may think there is no connection between the two events, I only wish I could feel so certain.

Chapter Six
Going for a Song

IT WOULD BE NO EXAGGERATION if I said that the television programme *Going for a Song* had changed my whole way of life. At the beginning of this book I described how I came to be involved in that programme, and if I was a little dubious about it all in the beginning I very soon realised that I would not have missed it for the world.

I believe the real reason why that show became an overnight success was that we showed, handled and discussed quite humble items, such things as a Staffordshire cow cream jug, things worth £30 or £40. I think that because it started in that humble way it made many people remember the things that their mother, or grandmother had, and they could go and identify many of the things that were shown in the first year or two of the programme. So, everybody began talking about *Going for a Song*. 'Did you see that jug last night? We went home and God bless my soul, there was one in our larder.' Now, that's how it was born and that's how I think it really became so popular. In later years it all became rather grand and I'm not so sure it benefited from that. Don't misunderstand me, it's always nice to see and handle something very nice and very rare, but to show say, the only known piece of horse armour in England worth £30,000 or £40,000, to viewers, well I'm not so sure that sort of thing held their interest so much as perhaps an asparagus tureen might have done. A Chelsea asparagus tureen was shown one day, and about a fortnight or three weeks after, a woman rang up to tell the BBC that her mother had such a tureen, it was cracked, but what should she do with it. It was suggested to her that she might send it to London for auction. She later wrote a very nice letter to the BBC to say that her cracked tureen had raised something like £350. How delighted the woman was. It made me feel that we were really getting home to a lot of people, whereas in the latter stages of *Going for a Song* it became so grand that it became more a spectacle to watch passively. I enjoyed it most when it was really something to watch and listen to, giving encouragment to people to go and search, and perhaps find, some of the more ordinary but most interesting things that appeared in the programme.

From the very early days, the chairman of *Going for a Song* was Max Robertson, and he had quite a number of things to look after during the show. Max had to sit at a desk between the four people taking part. There were three or four tiny TV monitor screens about three inches square which he had to continually watch. One screen would show him the estimated value of the particular article that was being shown, another the correct and exact description of the various articles so that he could prompt, say when we were incorrect, and also keep the programme to time. I must say I was very surprised to see how exacting the keeping of time is for all BBC programmes. Today they do not seem to go out 'live' quite so often as they did, but my word, they are timed to the very second. So Max, with that jovial expression of his on his face was really working very hard, listening to the comments of the four different people, watching the time, seeing we were talking sense according to the description he had, seeing what the price was, asking for their various valuations and so on. Max always had a most intense half an hour. Although the BBC stated quite emphatically that these items were not known or shown to us before the programme, maybe there were some viewers who wondered if it was possible by some means for us to see the objects before the programme started. I can assure you the objects were always completely hidden from every single person. You may be sure after all those number of years, I might possibly have some inkling where the various things were stored, but it was impossible to get anywhere near them. Don't think I was trying to cheat, but in a sense every programme was more difficult than the last. That may seem a funny thing to say, but the programme got like that, I really began to get nervous, thinking I should make such a fool of myself on one of those days. I wished I had some idea whether we were going to see glass or china or silver or plate. I knew we'd always get one piece of furniture so I wasn't too worried, but nevertheless, I would have enjoyed a peep at what they had in store for us!

I had a marvellous watching brief on *Going for a Song*. When some piece of silver came around which I thought was quite nice, how wonderful to have sitting next to me a man like Arthur Grimwade of Christie's, who just cradled it in his hands and spoke about it as though he'd known it for years. I was absolutely fascinated by the knowledge of some of these people. Listening to Arthur Grimwade on silver is something that sticks in my mind very much, another would be Earl Vandekar, still in business today with his tremendous knowledge of Chinese porcelain, and one could go on and on with such names.

I well remember the late James Kiddell, such an extraordinarily nice man, so willing to give all his knowledge away to anyone who showed the slightest interest, he was really the number one authority on porcelain. Jim Kiddell will be remembered by thousands, for he was a director of Sotheby's and had joined them as a boy. In a similar way the BBC also invited his opposite number from Christie's, a Mr de Boulay. All these people and many others I found were the complete tops in their particular fields, so easy to talk to and so willing to impart their great knowledge. Mr de Boulay although he retired from Christie's some years ago, was the man who went to play tennis one Sunday afternoon with some friends at a country house and discovered a Chinese blue and white bowl which was being used as an umbrella stand. My word, that must have been a lucky day for those owners because it eventually sold for a record six-figure price.

Another young man I got to like very much was Christopher Brunker, a young man who always sported a beard. He was also with London auctioneers, and was and is a remarkable expert on arms and armour. You know, it was quite extraordinary to sit in that programme and suddenly have some funny looking object come along that would go to the fellow in front of me who would say, oh this is a so and so, about 1590 to 1600. I used to sit and think, God, how do these people get all this knowledge. Young men, old men, but all absolutely supreme in their fields. Of course, Brunker became known most affectionately in the trade and by his friends as 'The Armourer'.

Apart from being amazed at the knowledge of the various men and women who have sat next to me on occasions, I had the same feelings towards some of the customers, as they were called, the amateurs who came to take part in the programme. One man I remember was the folk-singer Roger Whittaker. On one particular programme he took part in there were a couple of clocks, a bracket clock and a mantle clock and, here again, I was absolutely amazed at his knowledge and enthusiasm. Speaking with him afterwards he told me that he had always been interested in clocks and watches. I really complimented him, because it was obvious to me that he couldn't have had the slightest idea what he was going to be shown, and yet he seemed so happy and so easy with those clocks.

Another person I knew well was Lady Dowty who was also invited to come down as a collector. If the collector managed to win the so called 'customers' competition for three weeks running, they became the recipient of a gift of some kind. Lady Dowty managed to do this, and was in turn given a small papier-mâché chair which I've seen many times since, and of which she is obviously very proud. The one thing that sticks out in my mind is the comment she made to me when she said, 'Oh, I was so nervous when I went on that programme.' Apparently she got out six or seven different books on various antique subjects and read every single page of them. I asked her whether she had got a question on any one of the books that she had read, and she said, 'Not one.' Lady Dowty had been to all that trouble, but nevertheless she managed to win three weeks running.

All sorts of interesting people came down and took part in the programme, musicians, industrialists, people who in their own walks of life were very successful, and most of them had quietly been collecting little bits and pieces for years. On other occasions I had been equally amazed at the lack of knowledge of some of the people who were brought down as customers or collectors. There was a young girl, most attractive, who didn't seem able to speak at all. When asked a question by Max Robertson, she said nothing. There was an old kitchen chair laying about in the studio at rehearsal and Max said to the girl, 'If I should ask you a question about that chair you must answer, otherwise there is no programme.' Yes, she quite understood that. 'Well, supposing this chair came up what would you say about it?' She said nothing. 'This is what I mean,' said Max, 'you must say something. What is it?' She said, 'A chair?' 'That's right, and do you know what it is made of?' She thought carefully and suggested wood, Max was delighted. 'By the way,' he said to her 'do you like antiques?' To everyone's amazement she replied, 'No, they don't make them now, do they?' We had an awful lot of fun on the programme just quietly thinking how foolish some people were, and I don't doubt for one moment that some viewers thought just the same about me.

Speaking earlier of Lady Dowty, immediately brings to my mind her husband, the late Sir George Dowty, the great industrialist, head of the enormous firm of Dowty's in Cheltenham. Sir George appeared always to be working on something new in engineering, speed and aeroplanes taking up most of his time and energy. Some years ago I was privileged to go to his home. He always seemed to be totally engrossed in his business and yet, quite quietly during his lifetime, he formed one of the finest collections of silver made by that great Huguenot silversmith, Paul de Lamerie. To meet Sir George and to be in his company one would hardly have expected him to produce a cream jug by Paul de Lamerie, yet he collected and loved the work of that most brilliant of silversmiths. Since Sir George has died I imagine the collection has been broken up, but I can imagine what joy he had when he left all his engineering and business problems behind him, just to be amongst a few pieces of silver made by the man whom he came to regard as his friend, Paul de Lamerie.

Going for a Song became a great talking point with all and sundry. Some of the questions I was asked were very difficult to answer, and I don't like to be bowled out in that sense. It took me quite a while to remember the composer of the short excerpt of music which introduced the programme and on which it concluded. The composer was Respighi, and it was taken from *The Birds*. The number of times I have been stopped in the street and asked why it was the BBC insisted on playing music over the lovely little bird in the cage that became the programme's symbol. 'Why don't they stop the music so that we can hear the little bird?' people have said; other people, no doubt, have wished the bird would stop chirping so that they might enjoy the music of Respighi.

Having no musical knowledge at all, apart from being in the choir as a boy, you can imagine how surprised I was when I was telephoned one night and asked if I would like to appear on *Desert Island Discs*. I said, 'Yes', and despite knowing the thoroughness of the BBC I was really astonished at what happened behind the scenes. Roy Plomley was there with two or three of my selections, things I wanted him to play for me, like Gracie Fields *Ave Maria*, the *Hallelujah Chorus* and others. I didn't realise that there were sometimes eight or ten or even more different recordings of each and every record I chose. When I was asked which ones I liked best, I got myself very involved but, of course, Roy Plomley helped me with everything. At the end of the programme one is allowed one luxury to take with them and so I chose a copy of Ralph Edwards's *Dictionary of English Furniture*. I was absolutely amazed the very next day, because Queenie was being telephoned continually by people asking, 'what was the name of that book your husband chose for Desert Island Discs, because we would like to get a copy of it'.

There was an interesting follow up to *Going for a Song*, because within a few months of it starting, a similar kind of programme was introduced on radio in 1966 called *Talking about Antiques*. For the first year or so John King was the chairman but since then Hugh Scully has been in the chair.

This is a programme where people are invited to send in a photograph of an antique to the radio programme in which their particular object is discussed by Bernard Price and myself. Here again, although the programme is highly successful, there are difficulties in talking about antiques from a photograph. For one thing, so far as furniture is concerned, and I suppose for that matter porcelain as well, it is almost impossible to determine age from a photograph. It is very difficult for Bernard Price to be able to say 'this is absolutely genuine' or 'this is a copy' without handling the object. Nevertheless, it has a really extraordinary following of people who enjoy it, for it has run on Radio 4 for the last fifteen years. Of course, as with all programmes in their initial stages, there were teething troubles with this one. I think it was generally thought that the programme would not take off too well as listeners would have no chance of seeing the things that we were talking about, but that was overcome when we described objects in detail. The BBC were also surprised, because as I understand it, the original series was for six programmes just to fill a gap, and here we are, Bernard Price and I, still talking about antiques in 1982!

The first producer of *Talking about Antiques* was Bill Coysh. He went on for a year or so until he retired to write on antiques. Then a young girl came along named Pamela Howe and she produced this programme in a quiet and most efficient and friendly way for the next ten or twelve years. Since then she has gone on to produce many literary and garden programmes. We now have another good producer in Sarah Pitt. Here again, I think the longer this programme runs the more difficult it will be for me. I do not know how it appears to Bernard Price, but it certainly becomes more difficult for me because so many things are being, as it were, duplicated. The number of times I've spoken about a Chippendale chair that is more or less the same as any other, maybe with many little differences but basically Chippendale! It becomes difficult to know what to say that is different from the other times you have described a similar chair. Of course, it has frequently been pointed out to me that not everyone is listening to all the programmes all the time, so they will not have heard many of the earlier descriptions. Other people like to hear similar descriptions given once more in order to refresh their own memory. Of course, we, that is Bernard Price and I, seem to have fitted into a very compatible partnership over all these years. At one time there were rehearsals for the programme. We would go into a studio and be asked, 'What are you going to say about this question?', 'What are you going to say about that?' Nowadays, we simply go into the studio, greet one another, have a joke about something and almost at once begin off the cuff as it were, to deal with the recording of the programme. I get an idea in my mind when for some reason Bernard Price is going to stop and leave me just a little bit to say, and in a similar sort of complimentary way I know there are bits about furniture he particularly likes, so I leave him to say those. Now there are no play backs and very few retakes, only a few coughs have to be edited out and a few 'Ers' and 'Ahs'. We have always enjoyed making the hundreds of *Talking about Antiques* programmes and in all that time Bernard Price and I have never, touch wood, missed a recording date together.

From one's first appearance on television, should a programme continue for any length of time, not only does one get hundreds of postcards and letters, but one also tends to get recognised wherever one might be. Perhaps you can imagine how surprised I was to be stopped in the street by various people and asked if in fact I was Arthur Negus. This happens perhaps more often now, but I'm also asked if I mind being stopped, and if it's a nuisance to me. In point of fact it is not. It's part of the job I suppose that one might get recognised, and where someone will say, 'Hello I enjoyed that programme last night', or 'I liked that table you had', or 'I didn't think much of it at all last night', that is grand – just two or three minutes talk or so. Yet there are some people who are apt to say, 'Are you Arthur Negus? Well, I just happen to have this little thing in my pocket. Would you mind telling me what it is and what it's worth?' Those sort of people can be a nuisance, expecting as they do that a person should always be on duty as it were, in the middle of the street.

It's a blessing that perhaps only one in a hundred does that, and whilst I no doubt try and tell them what they have, I wish they would let me go on my way with just a nice genial greeting. I go at different times to the Imperial Hotel, Torquay, where lectures and talks are given by Bernard Price and myself. One day when I was in York a gentleman said to me, 'You're Arthur Negus.' He said, 'I went to see you at Torquay, and wasn't the weather beautiful!' and I said 'Absolutely grand.' To my surprise he went on to say, 'Of course, I didn't go to any of your talks, I enjoyed the lovely weather from the balcony of the hotel!'

A funny thing happened when my wife and I went in a store in Plymouth and enquired of a young assistant how we would get into the basement of the store. The young fellow told us that he was going that way and that we should follow him. As we were walking along he looked at me and said, 'You do remind me of Arthur Negus but I expect you get a number of people come up to you and say that.' I told him that as a matter of fact they did. He looked at me for a long time and then said, 'A much younger version if I might say so.'

Another thing that happens as you become recognised, is the flood of requests you receive to give talks. People ask you to open fêtes, talk to Mothers' Unions, and various societies and organisations so, gradually, as the years went by, I found myself giving talks all over The British Isles. This quite astonished me because I had never spoken to any society before I appeared on television. Everything followed on after the first year or two of *Going for a Song*, everything flowed from there. I found myself going off and joining in that well-known introductory hymn or anthem *Jerusalem* at Women's Institute meetings all over the country.

Just imagine trying to choose the best baby at a baby show. Now that's a very good thing to ask a poor fellow to do who's interested in antiques only. There stand twelve proud mothers, each one having the most wonderful baby on earth, and some fellow like me has to go and pick out one of them. On such occasions you know full well that all the other eleven will, from that moment, be gunning for you. I've managed that sort of situation and I've also picked out the best pot of jam and the best marrow in a show. Now whether I've done it correctly or incorrectly I've no idea, but they were all happy occasions. Without *Going for a Song* I believe I should have lived and died not knowing the one hundred and one different things that happen in the country. All the great occasions I have had with village people or, as I recall, going in to Lancashire all around the cotton towns talking to perhaps fifty people. In some little hall at night they would bring along their pairs of brass candlesticks or a copper coal-scuttle, all absolutely burnished, not just clean. They brought these items for me to look at and talk about, people loving very ordinary things that belonged to their mothers or their grandmothers.

There were other occasions when *Going for a Song* was

staged in many fine houses in support of charities. I tried to go to all of them when it first started. They all had a happy side to them and I came to realise how kind and good so many people are in supporting a well-known local charity. I have been to lovely places such as Arundel Castle and Berkeley Castle, Haddow House and Scone Palace, Scotland. In all of them I was allowed a quiet walk round, perhaps the morning after the show, enjoying the lovely things that they all possessed. It really has been quite a remarkable time, you might say where do I go now? People still come up to me and say 'What a pity it all happened to you so late in life'. You must understand that something like sixteen years have gone by since I first appeared on TV and, although one cannot accept every invitation, I'm happy in the knowledge that I still get a large number of requests. Anyway, during those early years, the first four, five or six years, I found myself going two or three times a week all over the place and it became necessary to have someone who could sort it all out for me. In other words, I had to get an agent. I had no idea what agents really did or, in fact, who they were or where to find one, but someone found me. I had a man come to me in Bridlington, by the name of Robert Holland-Ford, he was an agent, and he'd come across the country to meet me and felt sure that I could do with his services. So it was that I became the proud possessor of an agent. I then realised that I had entered a completely different world, a world that I knew nothing about whatsoever, what they call the entertainment world. Believe me, if ever you should get the opportunity to join in this world, you will certainly need an agent.

There is another side of things, which must be remembered: all this time I was a person employed by the firm of auctioneers and estate agents that I'd joined years before, Messrs Bruton Knowles & Company of Gloucester. It was becoming

increasingly difficult to fit all my many activities in. After all,
I was being paid to look after the Fine Arts side of their
business from 9 a.m. to 5.30 p.m. five days a week. I found
that I wasn't doing this, simply because it was impossible to
get back from talks to be in the office at 9 o'clock the next
morning. I shall be forever grateful to my firm because,
although I was missing from their place of business several
days in each month, never once did any of the partners ask,
'Where were you yesterday, why weren't you in the office?'
This is something I shall never forget. I'm now a partner
with that firm, but at that time I was just an employee, in
the sense that it wouldn't have been unreasonable for anyone
to have said, 'Look, you only gave me three days last week,
what's going on?'

Yet another point to be kept in mind is that in 1965, when
all this started, I was then sixty-two and married thirty-nine
years, and the business of going about all over the country
really can play havoc with one's home life. In the event it
didn't really upset our home life too much for Queenie, over
the first six or seven years, went with me on most occasions.
It is due entirely to her that I feel I'm more or less the same
person today as I was prior to 1965 when all the publicity
started. It came about in a very ordinary manner between we
two. After the first two or three programmes of *Going for a
Song* we were rung up one Sunday morning, by a friend, who
said, 'Have you seen the Sunday Times?' and I said, 'No.
Why?' 'Because,' he said, 'there is a criticism written about
Going for a Song in it and you ought to see it.' So, of course,
I went out and bought a copy of the Sunday Times and, sure
enough, there was a review of *Going for a Song* mentioning 'the
grey-haired man who recalls memories of Sir Mortimer Wheeler.' Now, Sir Mortimer Wheeler as everyone surely knows,
had tremendous knowledge in that TV Programme *Animal,*

Vegetable and Mineral and I was extremely bucked to read such a comment. It was the first criticism I had every really read, and somebody had likened me to that great gentleman. I said to Queenie, 'Here, read this' so she read it. I said, 'Well,' and she said, 'Well,' and then I said, 'Well, what about it?' 'Well, Sir Mortimer,' she said, if you want any potatoes with your lunch today they are still waiting to be peeled.' Now that's absolutely true. How lucky I am to have a wife like that who would carefully guide me on the right lines in order to keep both my feet on the ground, this is what is so nice about it, especially as Queenie has had to give up all sorts of things. Obviously, there were many nights when I could not be at home but that has now stopped, and I'm away for only five days in every month. One's life does get disrupted but she has put up with it all. We have come through that period now, and I hope that I still take the same size in hats as I did in 1965.

Of course, one goes through a variety of thoughts and feelings as one gradually climbs the ladder, as it were, from talking to thirty or forty people, to perhaps talking to audiences of six hundred or seven hundred. I shall never forget when I was asked to go and talk in Harrogate. I got to the hall about 4 o'clock in the afternoon and the talk was to be at 7.30 p.m. As I walked round this enormous hall with the person in charge, I saw that doors of boxes were marked with the names of a whole range of civic dignitaries. I said to the fellow who was walking round with me, 'They won't come will they?'. 'Yes,' he said, 'we are completely sold out.' I must say I had a funny sort of feeling as to whether I would succeed in keeping seven hundred people interested. I was staying in a hotel immediately opposite the hall, and it was dark by half past four. As I was getting ready to go across, and thinking about what I was going to say, I saw a group of about twelve people form up at the side of the hall, although I'd been told that all the tickets were sold. It then started to snow, and I went across to these people and asked them what they were standing there for, you'll understand that nobody recognised me. I said, 'All the tickets are sold.' 'Oh yes, but there might be some returned', someone said. 'But it's snowing,' I went on, 'You'll get wet through, as a matter of fact I know this fellow and he's not all that good, I shouldn't stand here and get wet in order to go and hear him.' So I left them and whether they got in or not I've no idea. I never thought that people would ever stand in a snowstorm just to get in and hear me talk about bits of furniture.

On one occasion I was asked to go to Queen's University, Belfast and give four talks on furniture and the like, and whilst I was staying there I had a telephone message from Stormont. Would I like to visit Stormont I was asked. I told them I didn't really think I had time, the schedules were worked out pretty tightly, not finishing until 10.30 or 11 p.m. and starting again at 9 o'clock the next morning, and then I would be catching a plane back to Bristol. The voice at the other end of the phone said, 'What a pity, the Prime Minister would like to meet you and show you Stormont.' Well, how could I decline an offer like that? So Queenie and I went to Stormont. You've no idea how nice it felt to drive straight on, not round the sides of the main drive, but straight up to the front door of Stormont itself. There I met the Prime Minister, Captain Terence O'Neill who said he would take us on a tour of the building. High up in the ceiling of one enormous room was a magnificent ormolu chandelier of about sixteen or twenty lights. He saw me looking up at this and said, 'Do you like that?' and I said, 'Yes I do, it looks to me to be a lovely article. I suppose you couldn't have got it any higher?' 'higher', he said, 'Well,' I said, 'look where it is, it's so high

Left. Examining a piece of furniture with Roger Warner at *The Antiques Roadshow*, June 1981.

Below. *On the Road* with the yellow Rolls-Royce.

Opposite below. Angela Rippon, a presenter of *The Antiques Roadshow*, receiving some guidelines on antique porcelain.

Opposite above. An attentive audience at *The Antiques Roadshow* held in the City Hall, Perth, in July 1978.

Previous page. *Going for a Song*, March 1971. Arthur and Max Robertson show their appreciation of some fine English silver.

After three years absence, *Going for a Song* returned to the screen in 1976, with Max Robertson again in the chair. On this occasion (*above*) the guest expert was Julian Thompson, and the 'customers' Honor Blackman and Alfred Marks, while, (*opposite*) the resident connoisseur and Max Robertson examine a rare French games table.

Overleaf. A silver cream jug comes under close scrutiny.

Left. On the set of *Collector's World* with presenter Hugh Scully.

Below. Arthur and Bernard still enthusiastically talk about antiques, ten years after the radio series began.

Right. Arthur with fellow guest-speakers Denis Norden (left) and Kenneth More at a *Birmingham Post* literary lunch, October 1978.

Below. Dolls of every period and every place of manufacture have long been favourites with collectors. Here Arthur Negus handles items from the celebrated Betty Cadbury collection.

Above. A rare moment to take life easy, to relax with a book on antiques, and familiar objects close at hand.

Opposite. Captain R. G. W. Berkeley, Arthur Negus and Canon Gethyn-Jones at a bring-and-buy sale in Berkeley Castle.

Mr and Mrs Negus at home.

In 1980, Bernard Price suggested a television
programme with the title *Arthur Negus: A Life
Among Antiques*. Produced by John Frost and first
shown on BBC South, it was later given national
viewing. The magnificent chairs were on loan
from Wilton House.

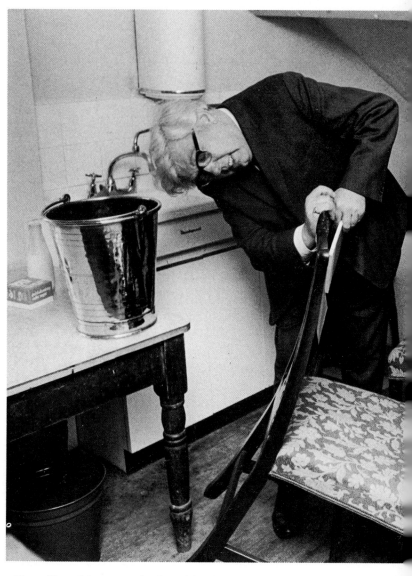

Above. Fine things may be found in the strangest
places.

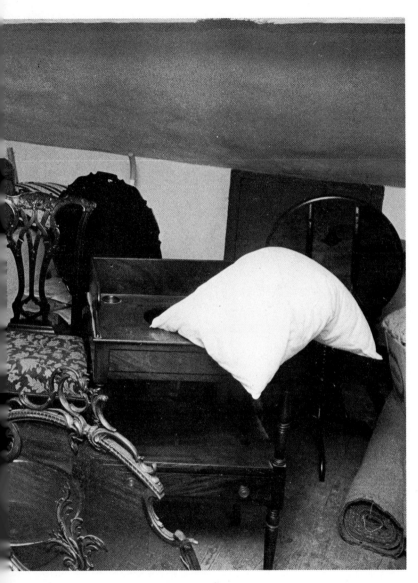

Overleaf. Relaxing at a friend's house.

it's impossible for anyone to see, are you sure you couldn't lower it?' 'I don't know', he said. Anyway, we passed on and saw other nice things and when we had more or less finished the short tour, a carpenter went by wearing an apron and Captain O'Neill said, 'Just a minute John, that big chandelier, is it possible to lower it?' The man said, 'Yes sir, that's on an adjustable heavy chain that can be lowered.' 'I see', he said. Later on, after the Prime Minister had gone, another Minister said to me 'You may rest assured Mr Negus the P M will have the chandelier lowered before the day is out.' I've never been back but I just wonder whether that chandelier is now more visible to people than it was before I went. It should really hang about eight or ten feet below the ceiling.

Anyone reading this book will know that I have made plenty of mistakes: one, however, occurred when I was examining a piece of silver on *Going for a Song*. This piece of silver really baffled me, for one thing I didn't know what it was, the second thing I didn't like it at all. One's own likes and dislikes can so often influence this business of appraisal and I am apt to say what I think. I said, 'I've never seen such a miserable object as this, the only thing this reminds me of is a child going down on the sands with a bucket and spade.' The object I was looking at was certainly silver, but was just like a little bucket, and so it all passed off like that.

When the programme was over I was told that I'd made an awful blunder, and the object was in fact a very rare early piece. The BBC were a bit bothered about what the owner might think. Well I could hardly believe it, so I rang up Arthur Grimwade and asked him if he had seen the programme. 'Yes,' he said, 'I did.' 'What about that child's bucket?' 'Oh,' he said, 'that is a very famous piece of silver, it is a holy water stoop, it's about 1692', and he went on in this vein and I gradually felt smaller and smaller. But there it is, it's not always that one can be correct in every detail. I found myself on *Going for a Song* in quite a different position to most other people who came on it. For example if they had a well-known silver man as a guest for the show they would have had a nice piece of silver for him to speak about. He wouldn't know what was coming, but he could guess he wouldn't be asked to speak about a piece of needlework. Now you see, where I sat, I used to come in on all these different things, and sometimes, incorrectly. I've only ever said that I like furniture, I've never called myself expert, clever fellow, or anything else. I do like furniture, and yet I find myself joining in with a chap who has got great knowledge of porcelain or great knowledge of silver, or a specialist in some form of the arts.

All sorts of different things turn up in the Fine Art world and I don't mind admitting when I have no knowledge about something I have been shown. There was in fact one occasion at the BBC when I refused to comment at all on one item. I just said that I hadn't a clue what it was. That bought some consternation, because at that point Max Robertson asked me to value it, and I said, 'Don't be stupid how on earth can you value a thing when you don't know what it is – you value it!' The programme was got through in that sort of vein, and of course, when it was over I was confronted by our rather irate producer who said they didn't really care for someone going on TV and saying they had no knowledge. I said, 'Well, it's no good, I had no idea what the thing was.' I further suggested to them there would be several thousand people watching the programme who would know exactly what it was and would know that I was just fumbling about just trying to find words. Well, I thought, I don't suppose I'll ever appear on *Going for a Song* again, but I did. When I arrived next time the very self same man who had been so critical of me said, 'That was rather a good thing you did last week, we've had so many letters which said well thank goodness the man down the end is honest.'

Now I feel a lot of people could benefit from that short story. Today young people seem afraid to say 'I don't know.' I've got so old that I'm not ashamed to say it, and I think that it's quite important that you should admit when you are beaten rather than try and talk yourself out of it, when hundreds and hundreds of people will know you are just messing about.

I'm sure everyone who took part in *Going for a Song* feels proud that nothing, well virtually nothing, was broken during the programmes. Some of those pieces of porcelain and glass, particularly when the customers didn't always realise they were in two parts, left me sitting there with bated breath. Yet one little thing did break in my hand, it was a Derby hyacinth pot. This was a little group of porcelain hyacinths set in a tiny porcelain jardinière, the whole thing about 7 inches long, and it was a bit difficult to hold with all those flowers and their narrow little stems. I laid it flat in the palm of my hand and showed it to the cameras. Suddenly, this little pot just jumped forward about a quarter of an inch and one of the little blossoms lay broken in the palm of my hand. One person wrote to me asking if I did in fact break the little hyacinths pot while it was in my hand. I had to admit to that damage but that was the only one. I discovered then how closely people watched *Going for a Song*. They didn't only listen to the programme, but they watched it intently, and it's quite remarkable what questions were born out of that programme.

For example, on one occasion I had a very early book in my hand, a book on gardening, and I was told to open the book in order to show the lovely woodcut border around an engraving of some sort of rose, and on the top of the engraving it said 'a rose without prickles'. I duly opened the book, showed it to the cameras for just a moment and said, 'Look at that lovely woodcut, just look at that nice engraving, "rose without prickles" ', and I closed the book. A girl from Cambridge University then wrote to me and said she had been watching the programme and could I tell her why the first 's' in rose was printed like an 'f ' and yet the 's' in prickles was printed in the normal way. Well, I had to find the answer to that. In the eighteenth century, particularly towards the latter part of the eighteenth century, the first letter 's' in any word was printed like an 'f ', and yet in any word that turned itself into the plural, like prickle to prickles, the 's' was written in the normal way.

Another thing, all my life I'd talked about Carolean chairs, meaning chairs that were made during the reign of Charles, when I had a man write to me a very nice letter pointing out that there was no such word as Carolean. He gave chapter and verse but I wasn't satisfied until I had a look in the Oxford Dictionary and, of course, there is no such word as Carolean. The word should be Caroline. I learned endless things from that programme.

When I refer back to the earliest programmes of *Going for a Song* I recall that after the first three I received a few postcards, not many but just a few, all written very nicely to me. You may remember that although I was only asked to go on the first and last of the six programmes, I was invited to go back on the second and third, and all subsequent programmes. For the first three I wore exactly the same suit, and my old school tie. After the third programme I received a letter which read, 'How nice it is to see an old school tie on the screen, you don't often see that today, but do you realise you've had the same socks on for three weeks!' Well, that wasn't quite true, but nevertheless this is what the lady thought. I had many postcards, funny postcards, curious letters, crazy letters. One lady wrote, 'Dear Arthur, I have a large chest I wish you could see it.' A headmaster of a school wrote to me and said that in an examination he asked the question who was the first man to discover that solid objects floated on water. He told me that he expected to read Archimedes, but in point of fact he said his brightest pupil had put Arthur Negus. So there are all sorts of funny sides to all of these things. I've had other letters which haven't been so nice, in fact I've had one or two that have been most objectionable, but you must expect that I suppose.

There was another side effect following *Going for a Song*. After it had been running four years or so, a man came down to meet me from BBC Publications and said I should write a book. The book would be called 'Going for a Song', but slanted towards furniture rather than all the hundred and one other things that had been on the programme. I had never written a book in my life and I didn't think I could ever write one, but here again, I got a lot of help from BBC Publications and from Max Robertson. They showed me endless pieces of furniture which I described and talked about, and tried to tell people what to look for, to determine whether they were antiques or copies. I talked about chairs, and stools, and tables, all in the same breath, and wall mirrors and wardrobes and anything else that came into my mind and all recorded on tape. Then eventually I got a transcript of the first tape. Well, Queenie and I sat together, and we read through this thing and we crossed out one thing and the other, when she suddenly said, 'They'll never publish a thing like this because the grammar is shocking, it's absolutely terrible,' so we agreed that we would put that right. We really went through it with a fine tooth comb, dotting the i's and crossing the t's, really making it grammatically correct. You can imagine how surprised and rather hurt we were when the BBC wrote back and told us they would not send us any more transcripts, because we had completely destroyed Arthur Negus.

So that was our first experience with transcripts or recordings for a book. It eventually got finished, and it was published in 1969, Max Robertson having been responsible for breaking the whole text down and putting it into chapters. The only thing I will comment on about the book is that no reference was made by me to any other book while I spoke into that microphone. It was straight off the cuff, and inside the covers might be the biggest load of rubbish ever written, but at least it was my honest to goodness experience and that, I feel, is not what is happening very often today. Now, it seems to me, that we get a spate of new books every year all on well written up subjects which are no more than cribs from previous editions of books. Every piece of furniture which is photographed in my book, I actually handled myself, and so it was a record of pieces of furniture I'd seen and handled and talked about. Books that are made out of other books are one thing, but the book that shows experience in a particular field is quite another. In recent years I've been invited to produce authors for a series of books that are being written today, and I've gone to people who had never written a book before in their lives, but are people who I know have tremendous knowledge. Believe me, they have produced some most excellent books on the six subjects that have been written about.

My dear wife also comes into the business of that book because neither of us had any experience of the book world. When the book was almost finished, a gentleman came from the BBC and said: this is the book, this is how it will be. We shall put a hard cover on it and we shall sell it for so and so. Turning to Queenie, he suddenly said, 'How many books do you think we should print?' Well she answered the question quite honestly by saying, 'I don't know, I've no idea about books, I don't know how many you should print.' 'You must have some idea,' he said, 'just for a first printing.' Then Queenie said, 'Well, four.' 'Four!' he said. 'Yes, four will be plenty, because I shall have to have one, we have two daughters and there is Arthur's secretary, yes four will be sufficient.' You can imagine the consternation that appeared on that · poor man's face, but there is nothing in that story except to prove once more that when you step into some other world you have no knowledge of it whatever.

In the event, the book the BBC published proved to be a best seller. It was all very pleasant so far as I was concerned, and I was very happy that all the people who had been involved in it had not been wasting their time. I had known nothing of the world of publishing then and I know but little more now, but it really was fascinating to watch it take shape and develop from a pile of paper into a real book.

There is no way that I might be described as a literary man. Of course I have written hundreds of thousands of words in catalogues and valuations, but that's very different to writing a story. There is only one novel that I can truthfully say that I have really enjoyed and that is *Sorrell and Son*, by Warwick Deeping, published in 1925; I have read that book many times. The only other books I like to have about me are a few reference works which I need to refer to from time to time. This is why I was a little wary when I was first asked to find authors for a new series of books on antiques. I was happy to choose them for the people they were and for the knowledge they had and to write a foreword to each of the six books that have so far appeared in the series.

What I did enjoy doing was going to some of the literary luncheons that were organised to help publicise the books.

The luncheons themselves proved to be very light, but I did meet some very interesting people, not only the literary figures who were there to speak, but from among the audiences who had come to listen to them. I must say that one speaker I did enjoy was Denis Norden. His radio and television scripts are always very clever and he has the happy knack of making very funny comments that appear to be completely off the cuff. At a luncheon in Birmingham he was describing the difficulties involved in marketing certain books, 'It would be easier,' he said, 'to try and sell the Pope a double bed!'

Chapter Seven
On the Road

WHILST *Going for a Song* was having its long run, the producer John Irving again came up with yet another novel idea which resulted in a new programme which I think had a most wonderful name, *Pride of Place*. It entailed John Betjeman and myself going into some fine homes, with John dealing solely with the architecture, and me with the furniture and some of the other contents. That programme had an initial run of, I think, six or eight programmes, yet it was never continued for a further series and to my mind it was one of the most successful programmes that I have been connected with on television. That may well show everyone that I know nothing at all about the content of TV programmes, but so far as I was concerned, to be with John Betjeman for a couple of days in, say, Hardwick Hall, and to listen to him go into raptures over the building was very rewarding. 'Hardwick, more glass than stone,' I can hear him now, revelling as it were, in the bricks and mortar that went to build that house. Then there were the wonderful Elizabethan ceilings, with everything shown in minute detail by the BBC who were going to infinite care in order to produce all the salient points that John would bring out about a ceiling or a cornice, or a cove. He was a great man to be with, full of fun, a great character John

Betjeman, and I'm only sorry that we didn't do more programmes together.

During the time that we were at Hardwick, Betjeman wrote
a poem about the farmers of England. I may have the facts
completely wrong, but I understand he sent the poem to the
Farmers Weekly but they didn't publish it because they said
they only published letters. So again, as I understand it, he
put 'Dear Sir' on the front of his poem and signed it 'Yours
sincerely, John Betjeman' and so it got published. There was
absolute uproar from the farmers about that poem, telling as
it did of the jaguars in the farmyards and the fact there were
no birds in the hedgerows. We used to come out of Hardwick
and walk down a little lane to a pub for lunch, and the pub
was full of John Betjeman and the poem. It followed the
hymn *We plough the fields and scatter* and soon the twenty-five
men and some girls in the bar, joined in such rousing choruses
as 'we plough the fields and scatter the poison on the land';
a really hard-hitting satire on some modern farming methods.
Shortly after we had left Hardwick Hall the magazine *Private
Eye* produced a small record which was a skit on John Betjeman and I going round these houses and that made a very
funny few minutes too.

It's always interesting to learn how anyone starts to collect
anything, and I once had to interview a man who was very
much in the public eye on that very question. I asked how it
was he came to be interested in antiques. 'What was the first
thing you ever bought?' I asked, and he said: 'Well, I used
to be a bank clerk and at that time I used to ride a bicycle
to a bank in London and I always passed an antique shop.
One morning I stopped my bicycle, for being fond of music
I had noticed in the antique shop window a bronze bust of
Paul Robeson by Epstein. I looked at that bust for a very
long time before I rode on. I was saving up to buy a car and

I'd got about £200. Several weeks later I stopped again and looked for the bust, it was still there. The owner of the shop called me in and said, 'I've noticed you looking in this window from time to time, you obviously like Paul Robeson.' 'Oh,' I said, 'I think he's absolutely marvellous, he's just going to break into song, just look at him.' Well, the result of that was that I came away with the bust, and for the next few years continued to ride my bicycle to the bank. 'That was the first thing I bought,' he said, 'I've brought it here to show you', and there it was and he was in raptures over it. That man was Lord Feather, better known as Vic Feather, former secretary of the TUC. I couldn't help sitting and looking at that man, a most powerful man, not in stature, but in the office he occupied. To think that all those years ago Vic Feather had ridden a bicycle for an extra two or three years in order to possess a small bust by Epstein. He said to me again as we sat there talking, 'Look at it, he's going to burst into song.' I thought, well, that's collecting.

I have been very lucky with so many of the programmes I have been asked to take part in. I never thought, for example, that I would one day ride about England in a yellow Rolls Royce, but that is just what happened in the TV series called *On the Road*. The idea of it was to trace the routes taken by the old mail coaches. One thing that particularly struck me as I was being driven along so very smoothly, was that there is obviously something very special about the appearance of a Rolls Royce. The driver said to me, 'You just watch what happens as we go through this main street.' Our speed was only about eight miles an hour, no speed at all, but every car which caught sight of us, pulled into the side, while we just floated on down the street. That was something I had never envisaged before, no one ever got out of my way when I was driving my little bull-nosed Morris Cowley.

So many interesting things happened during that series. What particularly sticks in my mind is a little village up the Great North Road which is now by-passed by the A1, known as Stilton. It looked to me as we drove down this village street as if it were completely deserted. Of course there were villagers living there, and the usual pub, and a very rusty petrol pump by the side of a disused garage, but there were also some enormous houses, really large houses. I discovered to my surprise that these were relics of the coaching age for, apparently, Stilton was once the crossroads of England, and those enormous buildings had once been hotels. It became the custom of these hoteliers to try and outdo one another in order to get more trade. When a coach put in there at night, one hotelier would offer free cheese and a biscuit before they started off on their journey in the morning. A whole variety of propositions were put up to the passengers, and in nearly every instance, cheese figured in the offers made. The cheese was made in Loughborough and the hoteliers stocked these cheeses and eventually when the demand for the cheese increased it became famous. That, I believe, is how these lovely cheeses came to be known as Stilton.

On the Road sketched out to people a coach journey starting from the General Post Office London, and it really must have been one of the sights of London to see the two dozen or so coaches, all drawn by horses of course, leaving in the evening for various parts of England. Our journey went from London to York and it was quite fascinating to delve into the old coaching days. The various sorts of things that I learned! For instance, children sing about 'Ride a Cock Horse,' but I had no idea what that meant, and I certainly didn't know what a Cock horse was, but I discovered as we went along. When we came to a huge hill it was explained to me that gipsies would have once kept a horse at the bottom of it in order to assist the four coach horses. They would hitch their 'Cock horse' at the front of the team and help to haul the coach up. When at the top, the gipsies unhitched the 'Cock horse' and were then allowed to offer their wares to the passengers before they trudged back to the bottom again to wait for the next coach to arrive. So I learnt a little bit about 'Cock horses' and also about the origin of the expression post haste which people use when they mean that they are in a hurry. Apparently you could send a letter, not by the ordinary mail coach which stopped at hotels, but by a rider 'poste haste' carrying the post. He would gallop like the wind for about eight miles to the next stop, then there would be a change of horse so that he could mount again and gallop for another eight miles to the next stop until the letter was delivered 'post haste'. All sorts of odd bits of information kept cropping up like that.

Not all filming days go well by any means. One morning it was decided that we should all have a very early call, the director had apparently been down to The Embankment on a lovely spring morning and had seen ducks swimming attractively about on the Thames. He could envisage me standing there with St Paul's as the background which might make an interesting picture. So we had a call at 4 a.m. and at 5 o'clock we were down at The Embankment, camera men and crews, all the lot of us standing there in the pitch dark. It was one of those days that never even got light, you couldn't see St Paul's, you could only just about see the ducks who were swimming on the river, and they had a great time eating the food we'd brought for them. Eventually, about half-past seven, it was decided that they had better take some pictures. We were all put in position and the ducks were swimming about as required, when the poor camera man said 'Well I can't even see Arthur, it's no good at all'. All was abandoned by the river and we all moved up to No. 1 London, that unique address of Apsley House and home of the Great Duke of Wellington, because that was one of the departure points for the mail coaches. It was a disastrous start to the day and one gets those days when not much goes right. The difficult problem for me was that I had to cross from St George's Hospital across that incredibly busy junction to No. 1 London. 'Walk leisurely across the road', I was told. You can imagine me walking leisurely, with buses, motor cars, motor bikes and everything else coming hell for leather all ways at me, so that was the next thing that went wrong. After about nineteen takes I did manage to get from one side of the road to the other. Then they decided to move on to Welwyn Garden City where there were certain things that had to be done, and it really meant that we worked on and on, it was midnight before I did eventually reach a hotel in Welwyn Garden City.

Back on the road we stopped off at one or two different places and met all sorts of people who were interested in coaches, the post, in penny blacks, and in pre-stamp covers. We were told the story of how they once used to 'send £5 notes by mail coach, but they only sent half at a time. The £5 note would be torn in half and the coach guard would deliver the one half to a certain address, wherever it was going, and the next day up would come the other half, and that's the way they used to send money about the country with some security. At one of our halts a man came up to me and said, 'Yours is a funny name, do you know anything about it?' I said, 'Well, I know it's a word in the English dictionary. As a matter of fact in Victorian days you could have gone into a pub and bought a Negus.' 'Yes, that's quite right,' he said, 'that's what interests me.' I told him the dear old Emperor of Abyssinia, Haile Selassie, was also called 'The Negus'. 'Yes that much I know,' he said, 'but do you know whether or not there were ever any silver bottle labels with the word Negus upon them.' 'I've no idea,' I said, but it did transpire that there are no bottle labels marked Negus because that drink, apparently, was not decanted. To my amazement this man then produced an old bill, a printed bill, in which someone had stayed in a certain hotel, and had paid about three shillings for his accommodation, and one shilling for the accommodation of his horse, but printed amongst the drinks, beers, ales, port and whiskey it also said, Negus. Negus was one shilling and sixpence so it must have been something. He kindly gave me that bill and I've got it framed and I wouldn't wish to part with it, but it's the only time I've ever seen the name Negus in print on a hotel bill.

Another thing that happened to me whilst we were 'On the Road' was when we went to Harrogate, to the Great Northern Show, where there were six coaches drawn by teams of horses. You must not lose sight of the fact that I was born in the middle of a town and I have virtually lived in the middle of towns ever since. I know nothing about what goes on in the country, shooting, fishing or hunting, and I was fascinated to see these coaches, all six of them, going on parade in that huge ring. I was suddenly asked if I would like to ride on one, so up I climbed and sat on the top seat, perched up high, with the driver. As we drove around while the judging was going on, I was fascinated to discover what a great understanding existed between the driver and each horse. To my amazement the driver talked to those horses all the way. He said, 'What are you doing Charlie, why don't you behave yourself, just look at you, now do go gently, just go along quietly, that's better; that's better. Jack, stop pulling that way, look straight to your front.' I'm blessed if those horses did not do more or less what this man told them to do, just like that, and that was something that I'd never seen ever in my life, never heard, and really knew nothing about at all.

'Jack that was beautiful, I'm proud of you', and so he went on as though he was talking to old chums, which I'm sure he was.

There was another TV series called *Collectors' World* with which I was associated on occasions. One programme sent me to Osterley, that splendid neo-classical house which is not many miles out of London. I really did enjoy that, for it is so grand and yet so simple. Everything in the house was designed by Robert Adam, and it is quite a remarkable experience. I have often alluded to Robert Adam and his vision of what we like to call 'the harmonious whole' in a room, but at Osterley everything there was just as I'd imagined it. Wonderful ceilings, and then you find yourself walking about on a carpet which actually copies all the features in the ceiling, a carpet that was probably woven at Wilton! I remember going into the eating room as it was called, and there were some magnificent chairs, about ten or twelve really wonderful armchairs, but there was no dining table, and that was something that puzzled me. Just outside the dining room door and hanging in a corridor, was a framed drawing signed by R. Adam, which showed this eating room as he had planned it. There were these lovely chairs all around the walls of the room, with an odd table here and there, but with no dining table in it whatever. I remember asking about this, and apparently a table was taken into the room on the occasions when that grand room might be used for a banquet, but in point of fact there was never any dining table kept permanently in the eating room, neither was it ever called the dining room.

Another house I visited in connection with the BBC, was Syon, a house about nine miles from Hyde Park Corner. I can well recommend anyone to visit this house because it is an old house modernised later by Robert Adam, and it's never been altered since about 1780, when Robert Adam introduced all his own ideas into it with fine plasterwork and Corinthian columns. As I was walking with the Duke of Northumberland, who owns it, along what was the Long Gallery, but is now the Drawing Room, I noticed that Robert Adam had blocked up most of the windows and put in lovely shaped niches. He had put Grecian figures in the alcoves and, of course, had introduced all the lovely swags, the bluebell drops, and lovers knots and ribbon ties all hanging down in splendid fashion, it was quite lovely.

In between the very long windows, I think there are as many as seven window-seats, having little shaped ends, and tiny seats that actually stood just below a dado in between each window. They too were by Robert Adam. I went across to one of them and said, 'That's rather extraordinary, you see this window seat doesn't actually fit in this alcove by about half an inch, that's a bit unusual isn't it?' 'Ah now, Mr Negus,' said the Duke, 'if you've got the time and patience, when they are all put in the proper places for which they made, all seven of them fit exactly.' 'Of course,' he said, 'they get pulled out by the cleaners who dust behind and keep it nice for everyone to see, but they don't always get put back in the same place. This was the method of construction in those days, everything had to be right, and maybe this is one reason why so many antiques survive in this country now, due to the skills of the eighteenth century cabinet makers.

Another thing I enjoyed doing, nothing to do with antiques, just the other end of the spectrum, were my appearances on that well-known Saturday night programme *The Generation Game*. This may seem funny, or even silly, but I used to take five or six antiques for the people taking part to guess their value. It started off with Bruce Forsyth, and I've actually been on every one of the series of The Generation Games, just appearing once each series. I must say, so far as Bruce

Forsyth is concerned, that he is a terrific worker, no question about that. All the time I was there from about 12 o'clock on a Thursday for the recording to take place at 8 o'clock at night, and which usually finished about 10 o'clock, he was there too, working away, suggesting this and suggesting that. Always trying really hard to get the programme across to the audience, with the success that it certainly came to have. Then came Larry Grayson as the programme's presenter, and here again, I was invited to his show. Although the programme continued in just the same vein the approach of the two men was completely different. Bruce Forsyth was effervescent, dashing about and working hard, while Larry Grayson achieved the same result by being just quietly efficient. They both seemed to enjoy every minute of it, and I suppose half the secret of that show, perhaps something like the Antiques Road Show, is the participation of the public. They are put through their paces to do all sorts of things and they enter into all these different games with such gusto, and everyone enjoys it. The cameras at the Road Show programmes are on the people more than the experts, and it is their reactions by word or expression which tend to make the programme so successful for the viewers.

Some of you may recall from earlier comments that I was once very interested in trying to play snooker. Some forty years ago I could, perhaps, play a good ordinary club game. In the series *Negus Enjoys* some people may have seen me with that great champion Ray Reardon, playing on a snooker table in which we showed old-fashioned cues and all sorts of old things involved with the game. One of the most remarkable shots in the game we played together occurred when I moved the ball, a red ball, above the centre pocket and invited him to go off the top cushion and cut it into the middle pocket as it came back. Ray said, 'Off of two cushions', and I said,

'Yes.' Sure enough, his ball went up to the top cushion and on to the side cushion, and the ball just brushed the red as it passed. In a jocular sort of way I said, 'No, not like that Ray, like this' and no one will ever believe it and may possibly think it was all concocted for the camera, but there it was, I struck the ball up to the top cushion, it came back and nicked the red into the middle pocket. Believe me, if I tried to do that for the next forty years I don't suppose I could ever do it again. I've been lucky enough meeting many people, and they excel in great skills in their particular arts like Ray Reardon, with his great skills in the game of snooker, a wonderful champion yet remaining always a very nice fellow.

One of the television successes of recent years has certainly been *The Antiques Road Show*. This programme has even succeeded *Going for a Song* in terms of popularity, it is extremely popular not only with the thousands of people who turn up wherever the show is held but also with the viewers. That part of it pleases me, but what pleases me more is to go to a recording and be able to meet all these people, and some of them are very funny. There are long queues of people, as a rule, and some dear old lady will come staggering in with a laundry basket full of crockery absolutely brimming over the top. Although there may or may not be a decent article amongst them, the enthusiasm of the old lady with her laundry basket and the fact that maybe only one thing comes out of it all worth perhaps £10 or £20 makes just seeing the joy on her face so rewarding. More so, perhaps, than when someone already has some knowledge of an article and knows they have something which is really nice, and is told it's worth £600 or £800. It is the more ordinary items that seem to attract me more to the people who own them. So many human things happen at these recordings. The idea is simply to get the owner's reaction to a particular thing whether it be good or bad. Some people come along with bright ideas that they possess something really wonderful, only to be told that it is worth practically nothing. They register surprise, sometimes just as acutely as those who receive a much more pleasant shock. It can be difficult to get reaction from some owners, but nevertheless it succeeds more often than it fails, maybe because of the huge variety of things that do turn up. That is why the programme is so popular.

As I watch the reactions of certain people, their great surprise, their disappointment and on the odd occasion or two, simply their greed, it all shows up so strongly on the screen. A large proportion of the people who come have little interest in the monetary value of the items that they possess, they simply come to be told whether what they own is or is not period. The fact that it might be worth money seems quite secondary to the fact that 'this was my mother's and has been in our family for many, many years and in no circumstances do I wish to sell it'. To my mind this is one of the most pleasant things that comes out of the programme.

Some might wonder why I have never appeared on ITV. This is simply because, after sometime on *Going for a Song*, I signed a contract with the BBC whereby my services were retained by them. I have never regretted this because, one way or the other, I have a great feeling for the BBC. It's difficult to explain, but I feel that the infinite care which the BBC exercise in showing such tiny details on pieces of silver, or porcelain or furniture, is perhaps one of the reasons why the programmes attract such an audience. After all, it is those extra details which often appear on pieces that make them so much the more valuable, and I think that is perhaps one of the reasons why the BBC are so fussy, and I use that word in the nicest possible way. Perhaps it all started with the antiques that first appeared in *Going for a Song*. There you had experts who laid particular emphasis on perhaps a tiny flower, or a tiny mark, and it became necessary for the director to go to endless trouble with re-lighting the whole thing in order just to show for one brief second that tiny mark of that particular flower head. So, maybe that pioneered the idea, because there is little doubt in my mind that any detail that I particularly asked the BBC to reveal, when I did eventually see it on the screen, was shown to absolute perfection. I feel that if viewers are enthusiastic enough or interested enough to remember some of the specific points that are made and are shown, they in turn might go and look likewise at such articles, and this is the way knowledge is disseminated.

On one occasion the *Antiques Road Show* went to Stoke, and in the time we spent there, some of the programme was recorded from the Spode porcelain works. During the afternoon it was necessary to record the introduction to the programme, and we showed one or two pieces of their marvellous porcelains from the factory's private collection. It just happened to be one day before our 51st Wedding Anniversary, and someone who knew this leaked the fact to the Managing Director of the factory. At about 4 o'clock the following afternoon, when the Road Show had closed its doors, the Managing Director appeared with a flat package under his arm and came up to me and said, 'We hope you like this, we have made it today.' It was a porcelain plate commemorating our 51st Wedding Anniversary! One often hears of people possessing things of which there is only one, but I'm absolutely sure that this plate falls in that category. This is the only plate bearing such decoration and inscription, and it really was a remarkable thing to have given us. I asked how many people had been involved with the production of this one plate, and was told at least fifty. In the morning it really had started from a lump of clay, and by 4 o'clock in the afternoon everything had been completed. That's just one thing that I think will always stay on our sideboard.

A series which I must say I liked being involved in, was called *The Story of English Furniture*. This was the title of a book written by Bernard Price in which he didn't discuss furniture as such, but revealed how the history, habits and customs of the English people dictated to some degree the types of furniture that were required and made through our history. For example, we started off in the very early primitive days, and there again, it's easy enough to be told how the old craftsmen turned chair legs with a pole lathe, but it is in fact a very different thing to see one working. In that very first programme, there was a man turning chair legs with the help of a piece of string tied to a 'whippy' branch of a tree, which when it was released produced the power that could actually turn a chair leg. Now that was something I had read about for years and never seen. The BBC as they always do, went out and found some of the nicest bits of period furniture from all over England and brought them into the studio just for me to talk about.

The one and only criticism I might have had of that programme, was that the pieces of furniture were so great and rare that each programme had far too many pieces in it, when I could have spent most of the time on any one of the fifteen or twenty pieces they had brought there. That programme gave me much pleasure because the items of furniture were so very, very, special. At the end, if one thought about it, the programme showed how the development of furniture occurred in the very early stages when there were only turners and joiners, and no cabinet makers; how certain Kings came to the throne, how foreign cabinet makers followed them and for the first time taught English joiners how to veneer, and how to cut marquetry. Everyone who watched those programmes saw all these things actually happen. It really is a great book, and the BBC produced a great programme from it.

There was one thing that happened two or three years ago that really amazed me. I became a Freeman of the City of London, and that was an honour that I feel more than proud to have. It seems to me that it may have been given to me as being representative of the *Going for a Song* programme. Needless to say, we have the certificate framed and it is a thing I prize very much indeed, maybe given to me as a token of the work that had been done by everybody in *Going for a Song*. Soon after that, Max Robertson and I did a charity *Going for a Song* in Colchester, for the Lord's Taverners, and we in turn were invited to become Lord's Taverners. The Taverners are a most amazing organisation who work only for charity, and when I say work, I really mean work. These people astound me, comedians who work hard all their lives, continuously appearing, perhaps twice a day, once in a theatre and once on television, finding time to go to charity cricket matches on a Sunday when they are unwell. I could mention names, one would be that great comedian Eric Morecombe. I'm sure he won't mind me talking about him.' I met him at Badminton one glorious Sunday when the Lord's Taverners played the Duke's Eleven, yet here was a man who was obviously ill. I sat and talked to him and said, 'Don't you ever stop, why don't you rest from all this travelling about?' He was telling me how he was going North the following Sunday, and he simply said, 'Arthur, I'm on borrowed time and if I can be of any help to any decent charity then I'm delighted to be able to do it.' It's quite a privilege to be amongst these sort of people who virtually have no time at all, and yet do find endless time to go to so many of these charitable events and give their whole-hearted support to them. There's no doubt about it, the Lord's Taverners are just brimming full of people of that ilk, so I'm delighted to be a Lord's Taverner, although I truthfully am not a very good one.

At the end of one series of the *Antiques Road Show* I was caught with quite a violent pain in my stomach. A doctor was called and I was taken very quickly into a nursing home. The first thing that the surgeon said when he looked at me was, 'I've never seen a man so completely dehydrated as you, you are absolutely dehydrated.' Half the cure that followed was that I drank gallons and gallons of water every day. That just shows how one can go on and on with a programme when one is involved. I didn't have the slightest idea that I was in fact gradually becoming ill. As the surgeon stood at the foot of my bed, he said, 'You are really overweight aren't you?' 'Yes,' I said, 'I know that.' He said, 'You are a good stone and a half overweight but you seem to have got a frame that can carry it. If I were you I don't think I'd take too much sugar in fluids, I'd give that up altogether it might be a help to you.' Then he said, 'Well perhaps at your time of life it doesn't matter.' I felt that was a very comforting remark to hear.

You know, there is a most rewarding side to being on television. So many people seem to want to meet Arthur Negus. It's curious really, because I can't understand why, nevertheless, many people do come up and say, 'Are you Arthur Negus?' and we just pass the time of day and that's most pleasant. Every now and then, perhaps every three months someone comes up to me, and I well remember a lady coming up in this way. She said, 'You'll never know what you did for my husband.' I said, 'Really?' 'Yes,' she said 'he died of cancer, and in the last three months of his life the only thing he lived for was *Going for a Song* and the pro- grammes you were in on the radio. He used to listen to all of those and he really enjoyed them so much, they were the only things he looked forward to.' That really makes up for all the running and tearing about the country and losing so much sleep.

Of course, like everyone else, I get one year older every year. I always used to drive my car to the town where the *Antiques Road Show* was to be held. I would drive up the day before, go on parade as everyone still does at about 9.30, wait for the opening at 10 o'clock when so many, many people would then descend on us in the hall, and stay there all day long until the hall closed. Then there would be a special 'goodbye' to be rehearsed and the recording might go on to seven or even eight o'clock at night. So that meant staying the night away, or driving some one hundred miles late at night and all this really taxed me too much. Now, however, I'm taken by a BBC car to these various towns and the car waits for me and brings me home at night. Although I have driven a car for so many years I had no idea what a difference that would make to me. To be taken to a town and do the road show and then be brought home, no effort to get there or back, just makes it very pleasurable, instead of what had become very hard work.

If you happen to be on television, you get into quite a different world where you seem to be at the beck and call of most newspapers or their reporters who want to interview you, and at first it came as a great shock that anyone should want to interview me. It was a thing I had never met before or expected ever to happen, and I used to feel quite bucked when someone rang up and said they were from such and such a national newspaper and could they have a talk with me. I would say yes, of course, but I discovered I didn't care so much for these telephone interviews, and in point of fact that is one thing I will not give now. I found I didn't have much recollection of what I had actually said over the phone to the people who asked me questions. So now I only give interviews to people provided that they are willing to come and see me, and can sit and talk to me. I find they take down exactly what I've said under those conditions and that gets reported properly.

The whole business of recognition in the streets, when you think you are well known, can be rather comical. I had a woman come up to me once and she looked a bit cross, and she said, 'You'll excuse me, but I've had an argument with my husband, you are who I think you are, aren't you.' I said, 'Yes I am' and she went over to her husband, and in quite a nasty voice, said, 'I knew I was right, I knew it was George Cansdale.'

Another story in that vein was sent to me by Arthur Marshall. He is a gentleman I have yet to meet but he must be a most excellent fellow to be able to tell this story against himself. He is the chairman of one side of that panel which plays the TV game *Call My Bluff.* He wrote and told me how pleased he was when someone stopped him in the street and said, 'You are Arthur?' He replied that he was, feeling, he said quite bucked about it, fancy being recognised after only three or four appearances. The person then said, 'Would you kindly sign my daughter's autograph book?' and so he signed his name, Arthur Marshall, and handed it back to the lady, who looked at it and said, 'Oh dear, you are not Arthur Negus, you've spoilt my daughter's book!' Now for a man to have been able to write a story like that he must be the grand fellow I'm sure he is.

I was once asked if I would make an appeal on the radio in order to help backward children. I agreed that I would and there was a fair bit of preparation for this, because I insisted on going and seeing the actual place that I was going to talk about. I wanted to meet the children who were in there, and I wanted to see the people who looked after them. When I found everything to my entire satisfaction I agreed to do the appeal. It really is most extraordinary, because you can become most apprehensive about doing such a thing. Anyway, I got an idea of what I was going to say, and had certain particulars given about the children's Home. Then the great day arrived and I made the appeal. After it was done my wife said, 'Supposing nobody sends anything'. 'Oh my God,' I said, 'think of that!' So we immediately wrote a cheque for a fiver and sent that off. I could envisage perhaps, if one hadn't got the right approach or the right appeal for people to send money to a charity, that such a thing could happen, which would be an absolutely disgraceful thing. The thought certainly went through our minds, so we at least made sure that there would be a fiver in the kitty.

Several of the shows I did for charity in theatres and halls up and down the country, were produced by Bernard Price who often used closed circuit television. This meant that all who came to support their favourite cause had the opportunity to see small objects in detail, just as though they were watching TV at home. The most successful event of this kind was without doubt the *Going for a Song* we did at Arundel Castle, home of the Duke and Duchess of Norfolk. It was in aid of the King Edward VII Hospital at Midhurst. I shall never forget that day, 29 November, 1969, for it began to snow heavily during the afternoon and didn't look as though it would ever stop

We all began to wonder if anyone would ever turn out at eight-o-clock at night in such appalling weather, but in fact it deterred very few. The Baron's Hall where the evening was held just glittered with light, ancient family portraits, and fine furniture. Above all, the huge fireplaces were full of blazing logs and it was all just as I imagined an old English Christmas would have looked in a great castle.

Meeting the late Duke of Norfolk who, as Earl Marshall, had been responsible for the organisation of so many spectacular State occasions was a great honour. It was not until I met him that I realised what a truly great man he was and what a keen sense of humour he possessed.

His flair for organisation showed itself even in this special *Going for a Song* for which he was chairman. He gave me a timetable to enable me to arrive on stage at precisely the right moment, eight-o-clock. I followed it all to the letter, and the moment I stepped onto the stage a castle clock struck the hour. It was a great evening that I shall never forget.

So many well-known people always seemed ready to give their time for fund raising. Lady Isabel Barnett was always a great favourite with audiences. So too were Millicent Martin, David Jacobs, Cyril Fletcher, and Leslie Crowther, it always made things so easy when working with such professionals and I'm grateful to them all.

Chapter Eight
Home and Away

WHEN I WAS A BOY, we had two large cellars under the shop in Reading, in fact they were as big as the shop and workshop put together. You could barely move in those cellars because they were full of timber and half pieces of furniture. My father would say to me 'Now go and put that piece of mahogany downstairs, it's such a lovely colour and one of these days it will come in very useful.' He was a great chap for matching up colours without disturbing the surface of the wood. When I came home from school he would sometimes say, 'Oh just a minute, come in and saw this lump of wood will you, I have marked it.' He had put a line right across the mahogany top of an eighteenth-century breakfast table. Such a thing would be sacrilege today, but then, in about 1920, you could buy them from fifty shillings to five pounds and not be able to sell them. After I had sawn the piece off, he'd say, 'This will make lovely bracket feet, it's such a beautiful colour.' Another thing I had to do, was to cut fret-work designs in quarter-inch thick Spanish mahogany, to be used as ends for wall brackets. I used to use a small fret machine which cost about thirty shillings in those days. With that fine little fretsaw I used to pierce the ends in the Chinese Chippendale manner, and because the wood was so hard and of such lovely quality, the friction of the saw itself seemed to polish the cuts, and there was no trouble in polishing up the ends. He used to make these up into hanging bookshelves, with two little drawers under, with the nice Chinese Chippendale style pierced ends. After he died I found a couple – two that he never used, but which I had certainly cut because I cut all the fret ends. I took them and made a set of shelves, but I'm afraid it's not like the ones he made. I often look at it, because I've still got it. Certainly it's a Chippendale-style hanging wall bracket fitted with two drawers with fret ends, but it lacks the sort of finish that my father would have given it. It's the one and only piece of furniture made solely by Arthur Negus, and it hangs in the hall of our home today.

There is little doubt in my mind that every home has got some sentimental things in it, that is if it is a real home. I am not particularly sentimental, but I have kept a very small thing that my father made. Apparently, when he was courting my mother, it must have been prior to the beginning of the century, he made a little grandfather clock. It is a miniature grandfather clock, and by miniature I mean about 12 inches high. He just made it and gave it to her when they were courting. This is one of the things we have that I would not like to part with, it's got no specific value, it's just one of those things.

Everybody, it seems, appears to think that we must live in an old house completely surrounded by extremely fine things. I don't think anything I possess has ever been on television, simply because I have not got anything that might merit that. When I stand in front of a camera and hold a rare Fabergé egg and say, well here is a most wonderful thing, then touch some hidden spring and up pop three miniatures and I say it's worth probably £250,000, as that particular one was, I think a number of people seem to think that it is mine. Of course, there never was a more mistaken idea. You might be surprised to learn that we have three plaster ducks in our hall, flying up the wall. When friends come in they might be thinking well fancy, look at those ducks, they must have cost seven shillings! There they are flying up on the wall, and the one that's farthest away is the smallest. I once said to my wife, 'I don't particularly like those ducks', and she said, 'No, well you've forgotten, haven't you, they were given to us by Hilary.' Our eldest daughter bought them from the very first money she ever earned as a nurse at St Bart's hospital. Now, of course, that puts a different complexion on those ducks. In the open market they are worth nothing, but I trust they'll never leave the hall where they are now because they mean that much to Queenie and me.

I have been very lucky with miscellaneous things that I've been given over the years, and sometimes they have come in a rather funny sort of way. One in particular is our pair of . French porcelain cornucopia. These were in one of my firm's auction sales about twenty-five years ago, and I said to my wife, 'There's a lovely pair of French cornucopia in a sale we've got in about a fortnight, I'm going to try and buy them, they are so pretty that I'm sure you'd like them.' Well, she went to the sale on the view day, saw them, and liked them. Later in the day, a friend of mine who was quite a wealthy chap, came up to me and said, 'What about that pair of vases then?' 'Oh,' I said, 'you mean those French cornucopia, they are absolutely beautiful.' 'I thought they were,' he said, 'well, you buy them for me.' 'How much do you want to give for them?' 'You just buy them,' he said, 'I'd very much like to have them and I shall give them to my wife.' So, of course, with no more ado, I bought the pair of cornucopia for him at the auction. On several occasions Queenie and I went to their house to dinner over the years, and I always noted what I called my pair of cornucopias, stuck up there in a cabinet, and eventually I told them the story. He said, 'Oh, you were so silly, why didn't you tell me, I wouldn't have bothered about trying to buy them.' 'Oh no,' I said, 'I'm there to see that the best price is got and I'm quite happy about it.' Well, after some years his wife died, and the very next morning, quite early in the morning, this man came to the door of our flat with a fish basket, and wrapped up in the fish basket were the pair of cornucopia. 'I've brought these for you because I'm sure Ethel would want you to have them,' he said. Naturally we do still have them and trust we always will.

When we got married my wife said that she would like a tallboy, so I said, 'Oh I'll buy you a tallboy,' well I never did, but some ten or fifteen years ago in a house at Badminton a magnificent tallboy was coming up for sale. Of course, I came home in just the same way as I did with the cornucopia, and said, 'I'm going to buy that tallboy, at last I've seen one I like.' The self same thing happened, a lady came up to me and said, 'What about that tallboy?' 'Oh,' I said, 'it's beautiful with its original set of brass rococo handles.' So she said, 'well, buy it for me' and I said, 'How much do you want to give for it?' It was just the same story: 'Just buy it' she said. So I bought that tallboy, all those years ago, for about £60 and it went to her home. There again, eventually they were told the same tale, how I'd shown off to my wife, how I was going to buy it for her. Nowadays I have free entry to that house, 'Never go by,' she said, 'never go by without you come in and see your tallboy.' It still looks lovely and such memories are very pleasant.

I have already mentioned our daughters Hilary and Anne. You will remember that both of them had taken up nursing. Hilary eventually went nursing in South Africa where she married and had two children. Her husband, Ray, was a wattle farmer, and we didn't have much idea of what that was, but Queenie found out when our first grandchild was born, for naturally she went out there for the birth and christening. Wattling, apparently, is a continuous planting of trees over a seven year period. When the young mimosa trees reach maturity the bark is stripped from them during the seventh year of their growth and is exported to England for tanning leather. These trees are then cut down for new planting, and all the wood goes to some huge factory out there, Lion Match was the name of one I particularly remember. Since that time over thirty years ago, Ray has had a heart attack, and has now bought a farm which he thinks will suit him better, a banana farm. We are often asked if Hilary will ever come home and the answer is simply no, because her home is quite definitely in South Africa.

Of these two grandaughters of ours, one has married, and has in turn also produced two daughters. So during Christmas 1980, the great day came when we went to South Africa and stayed for about five weeks in order to make our introductions to our two great grandchildren. There is one story which my grandson will hate me saying, but this elder great grandchild had obviously had it so impressed upon her that her great granny and her great grandad were coming. One day I found her looking out of the window because Richard, my grandson, was flying down from Johannesburg where he is now, employed in a Bank, and was flying home for Christmas. I said, 'Julia, who are you looking for?' and she said 'great Richard'. Now 'great' Richard is about twenty-five, and that title has stuck to him forever more in our family, poor Richard will always be known as 'great' Richard.

Anne, in turn, married a young fellow named Roy, home on leave from Malaya. They have a family of three: Richard, Michael and Deborah. So what with Ray and Roy we were all right. Later we visited them in Malaya where Roy was a dredge master. He dredged for tin, working from one of those huge dredging boats with an endless chain of buckets coming up out of the water. The tin is actually refined on board the dredger where they have an armed guard, because tin is worth so many hundreds of pounds a ton. It was quite remarkable to go on board this huge vessel and see the buckets bringing up sludge from the bottom of a lake and seeing it refined, the little grains of tin kept and the rest of it all thrown back. Roy explained to me that the level of the water never increased or decreased, the sludge went back to the bed of the lake and remained the same as it was before they fetched it out.

There is just one thing that makes Queenie and I feel rather sad, not that our daughters married, of course not. We saw them in their bridal dresses and trousseaus but we never saw either of them married. We visited both the girls at different times. Out in Malaya, while walking along a lovely sandy beach in Penang, which I thought was far enough away to be left on my own, when, bless me, if a couple didn't come up to see me and say, 'Surely not Arthur Negus', I said, 'Well, I never did!'

Something of a similar thing happened in South Africa when my son-in-law saw in a Durban bookshop, a book that I had written, how it got there I haven't the slightest idea. Ray became so elated he wanted curbing a bit, he went to the shop assistant and said, 'You see this book *Going for a Song*; it was written by Arthur Negus, and here he is. The same thing happened one day when we visited a huge Safari Park, we were walking along a catwalk over a pit in which there were bears and all kinds of animals. This catwalk was a little precarious for it certainly swayed about a bit. At the end there was a gate, and sure enough, as we came up to this gate it was opened for us, and a man said, 'Always a pleasure,

Mr Negus', I thought, well of all things, just fancy, miles away in South Africa.

Roy and Anne took their two sons to Canada where their daughter was born. They had gone to Canada gold mining, and while Roy was working in the mine a piece of metal flew up and he lost the sight of his right eye. They returned once more to Malaya before eventually coming back to England after an absence of some twenty-five or twenty-six years. The two families have managed to provide us with five grandchildren and two great grandchildren, so we are very happy about that.

While Roy and Anne were in Malaya, they sent the two boys back to be educated in England at Wycliffe. We often talk of the happy times we had, because with their parents in Malaya, their home was at our home. They came just whenever they liked, we had them for two of the three holidays to start with. We also attended every function at the school that we were allowed to, the other boys had their parents and these two just their older grandparents. So we went to the concerts, the plays, and the sports days; I really think that there is little doubt that we enjoyed the young lives of our two grandsons more than perhaps we did with our own two children. I suppose every family experiences this.

In these later years how we enjoyed the opportunity of picking up that young life again and watching our grandsons in all their activities. Sports days were a particular pleasure, I remember one day when parents were advised by the headmaster that it would be nice if parents took packed lunches for the boys. Well knowing our two, and their capacity for food, and knowing full well that they were bound to bring back two or three other boys whose parents perhaps were abroad to have a dip in with us, Queenie really filled the boot of the car with every type of food possible. In no time at all that huge load vanished with about four or five boys really having a good tuck in. Suddenly a bell rang, and Richard, with his mouth still full of food, said, 'Granny I'm in this race I shall have to go', and he went running off to line up with about six other boys for a 400-yard race around the circle of a track. Believe me, the further the leaders got, so much further did he fall behind, so much so that the race was won and over and almost forgotten before poor Richard came in on his own, last. He was quite happy about it, because he came over and said, 'Granny I made a mistake, I've had too much lunch.'

Both boys could swim like fishes but perhaps Michael was the better swimmer. There again, we went to the swimming baths to watch the races and we happened to be sitting near the headmaster. He said, 'Now you just watch your grandson, he'll have finished four lengths of the baths while the rest of the people will be just about completing two.' Sure enough this lad went off and soon left them in his wake, that was one thing amongst others this boy could do. I suppose being born in Malaya and almost living in that lovely warm water around the coast there, it was absolute second nature to him, he really was a fine swimmer. I think it would be true to say that Michael did not really enjoy sports, the headmaster said he could really have been a wonderful swimmer if only he would practise, but he preferred not to apparently. Richard, on the other hand, was sports mad, he loved rugby and cricket, all of it. To get out on that sports field was everything and, with a school like Wycliffe, no doubt the coaches saw that he had some ability for rugby and so he became the recognised scrum half. We went to some of those rugger matches and whether they were played away, or when they played at home, we still enjoyed watching them, win or lose, as the case might be. Then, one day after a match we did not attend, the sports master rang through to say, 'We are sorry but we have got some bad news for you, Richard has broken his leg at rugby this afternoon.' 'Oh dear, oh dear,' I said, 'just fancy that, and his mother 8,000 miles away.' 'Yes,' said the games master, 'but I don't know what we shall do for a scrum half on Saturday!' For the first week or so he had a whale of a time. There he was in the headmaster's study, laying full length on a settee with his leg in plaster, from ankle to thigh, and everybody who visited him used it as an autograph book. He really felt grand about it, but after about six or seven weeks with this great weight of plaster it was no longer such a novelty having a broken leg. It mended well, and he played rugger for several years after that happened, and happily continues to do so until this day.

My wife had always been used to having dogs around her, so we decided to have a little dog, and we bought a black Scottie dog who we called Andrew. He was a great favourite with both of us, but quite definitely he was Queenie's dog, no doubt about that. I think it is generally well known that these dogs can be fighters and he certainly fell into that category. He never learnt his lesson though, he only had to see a big Alsation somewhere and he'd want to go and have a bite. I think he used to get the most tremendous hidings off the big dogs, but nothing stopped him, and when he'd got over one hiding he only had to see another dog and he'd have to have another go. It's extraordinary how one gets so attached to a dog. I remember on one occasion Queenie had to go into hospital and have an operation and, lo and behold, we, that is Andrew and I, were left in the house while Queenie was away in hospital. I used to go home at night and this little chap was so excited and so pleased to see me. I talked to him and fed him and walked him, and, of course, he never answered back but was, nevertheless, tremendous company.

When Queenie got better she went to Reading with some friends for a week's holiday and took Andrew with her. Oh dear, the difference then in coming home to a 'dead' house, it was absolutely remarkable. Formerly I went in and that little black Scottie came running up to me so pleased to see me. Then came the time when I used to open the door, and not a thing, nobody to talk to, no one to do anything for, well, I shall never forget what a terrific difference that little dog made. We had him from about three months old until he died. Then we went and got another Scottie and this one we called Hamish, and it was an extraordinary thing, because Hamish became my dog. He was another dear little chap, but he wasn't a fighter anyway, and he and I we got on well with one another.

Some years ago we moved into a flat in Cheltenham and Hamish moved with us. Every morning I used to take this little dog around the square, and every evening when I came home there he'd be waiting at the door for me to take him out again. How one gets attached to a small animal like the Scottie dog. Another thing that amazed me was the number of people who nodded and said good morning, and I'd say good morning to them on our little daily route march. Eventually, Hamish died, and so we are living for the first time in our lives in a flat and haven't a dog. One day, in another part of Cheltenham some years after Hamish had died, a young woman who was pushing a baby in a perambulator, stopped me and said, 'You don't remember me, but you used to say good morning to me every morning when I rode my bicycle to school, when you were walking round with that little dog.' Here now was a married woman with a baby. Everybody seemed to know me and that little dog, but poor old Hamish got very old and very slow. There were some buildings being erected in Cheltenham, and every day I walked by them and said 'how do you do' to the Irish labourers who were helping with the building, laying bricks and so on. One day a chap said to me, 'He is coming on nice and fine', because Hamish would be about twenty yards behind me, just walking slowly along. A really funny thing happened one day. My wife happened to be looking out of the window of the flat on to the lawns, and there was a little tiny Scottie dog, it had obviously got out of somewhere, and she saw it had a collar on. She ran downstairs, but by the time she got there the dog had vanished. So she ran along the road, passed the building site and said to one of the men, 'You haven't seen a little Scottie dog have you?' and he said, 'Blimey Mrs, he hasn't got away has he?'

After I had been launched into a whole new world, so far as I was concerned, of radio and television in 1965, Queenie and I found ourselves able to have some holidays abroad. Our first trip was a journey starting from Gatwick that gave us stops in Nice, Naples and Istanbul, before staying a week in Beirut. All of that time we had the same aeroplane, pilot, crew, and courier. That was really our first holiday abroad, it was particularly enjoyable because we formed a relationship with four other people who still remain some of our nicest friends.

Later we visited Rome, that most wonderful city, I think we spent the best part of three days inside St Peter's. We were asked if we would like to see the Pope, not a private audience, of course, but on certain Feast Days the Vatican is opened to perhaps two or three hundred tourists and pilgrims. Eventually the Pope arrived in the huge hall sitting on a throne and carried on the shoulders of several men. At the end of the hall he gave a short address which was repeated by the various Cardinals in almost every language in the world. When we walked inside the Vatican there were signs to be seen everywhere, 'no cameras', 'no cameras!' To my absolute amazement, as soon as the Pope, Pope John, was carried in, it was something like a boxer being acclaimed in the ring. He put his two hands above his head and sort of shook hands to either side as he was carried along, and there were thousands of people with cameras taking pictures. If the soldiers on guard in the Vatican saw you with a camera across your back they would take it off you, but as long as you had it hidden or carried it under your coat, well, there were literally hundreds taking snaps. All the flashlights kept flashing and Pope John seemed to enjoy every minute.

Venice is a city I much admire. The Doges' Palace being of special interest because I met so many good pieces of Italian furniture there. Unfortunately the furniture is not kept in the first rate condition that we would expect to see it cared for in the Victoria and Albert Museum, London. Of course, there were wonderful paintings too, but I regret that I get no enjoyment out of looking at paintings, I just don't know what they are about. We are not so strong on our legs now and I can't recommend Venice unless you are a good walker. You take a gondola or you walk, and there are a lot of bridges to cross with about twenty-four steps up and twenty-four down.

I like the sense of age that so many places have, the lovely island of Cyprus is like that. It was brought home to me so forcibly when I was looking at the remains of some early buildings, and a man suddenly said to me, 'Do you realise St Luke walked along there?' On another occasion we saw three priests, at least they were dressed as priests, but what intrigued me with them was the fact that they were just sitting on the pavement with their paints and brushes and putting the finishing touches to copies of fifteenth-century icons. I think if you wanted a particular icon of the fourteenth or the sixteenth century, it seemed to be that if you called back at the same time tomorrow, then the icon you wanted would have been prepared. I just wonder how many of those have been let loose in various countries all over the world, with people having bought them because they thought they were old.

People ask me now if there is anything at my time of life that I wish I had done, and the answer is usually no, yet on reflection there is just one thing. I suppose it stems from the fact that starting out in life with no capital at all, and watching the dealers in those days who were able to buy fine goods and pay for them when I couldn't have done, there is perhaps one thing I would have liked the opportunity to do. I would have loved to have been able to go to Christie's or Sotheby's, to one of their really fine furniture sales, and to have picked out one thing that I could have lived with. Then to have put a mark against it in the catalogue and sat there and bid, and bid, until it was knocked down to me. That's something that won't happen now, but that perhaps is just one thing I would have wanted to have done.

Would I do anything differently if I could have my time all over again? Well, as funny as it may sound, and on reflection, I don't think I would change one little bit. I was always in trouble at school, in those days I had the cane at Reading School as much as any boy, and yet I wouldn't have changed that; perhaps some of the happiest days of my life. I wouldn't have changed Queenie, we are getting on now, and you know if we manage to live to October 1982, we'll have been fifty-six years married. That in itself is quite something, and I'm sure no one would want to change that should it ever happen to them.

As for radio and TV, I have already said that I would not have missed it for the world. In spite of the occasional frustrations, which I am old enough to know are to be found in any job, I enjoyed every minute of it. How else could I have met so many interesting people, or had so many inviting doors opened to me? One thing which I never imagined for one moment would ever happen, could only have come as a result of the years of broadcasting. It came about in my eightieth year, when my name appeared in Her Majesty's Birthday Honours List for 1982, as a recipient of the OBE.

After I had got over the surprise, and what was almost disbelief, I also began to see it all as an honour to my family and the world of antiques in which I had spent my life. Goodness knows what my father would have said.

Above all, I still have all the old enthusiasm for anything which I like in the art world. It needn't always be a piece of furniture, although that is still my greatest love. I can admire a fine piece of porcelain, or silver, and I still get a thrill from going to a house for the first time: just to walk in the hall and to see a nice piece of furniture, and wonder what on earth all those other rooms contain.

Index

Figures in italic type refer to the captions to the illustrations.

Adam, Robert 88, 140–1
Antiques Road Show, The 70, *110*, 143–4, 145–6
Arthur Negus: A Life Among Antiques 7, *121*
Arundel Castle 152

Belton House *52*
Berkeley, Captain R. G. W. *118*
Betjeman, John *52*, 133–4
bicycles, story of the stolen 40–41
Birmingham Post 115
birthplace, Arthur's 12
Blackman, Honor *112*
Bradshaw, Lindsey *50*
Brown, Harold 24–5
Brunker, Christopher (The Armourer) 97
Bruton Knowles & Co. 43, 44, 61–74, 105–6
Bruton, Norman 62, 63
Buckingham Palace, gold and silver collection 75–7

Cadbury, Betty, doll collection *115*
Caroline chairs 128
catalogues, preparation of 61–2
charity appeals 151
Chippendale, Thomas 10, 87, 88
collecting interests: caddy spoon collection 36
Collectors' World 114, 140
Coysh, Bill 101

de Boulay, Mr 97
de Lamerie, Paul 99

Desert Island Discs, appearance on 100
dolls *115*
Dowty, Lady 98
Dowty, Sir George 99
Duccio case, the 67

East, Edward (clockmaker) 22

Feather, Vic (Lord Feather) 135
Forsyth, Bruce 141
Frost, John *121*
Furniture antique, identification of 14–15, 78–9
Chippendale 15, 24, 68, 82, 87, 88
Kent 82
Sheraton 82
twentieth-century, views on 83–86
Victorian 83

Generation Game, The appearances on 141
Gethyn-Jones, Canon *118*
Gillow, Robert 82
Gimson, Barnsley & Waals 85
glue pot, story of 14
Godmanchester 12
Grimwade, Arthur 96, 125
Going for a Song 7, 9–11, *50–51*, 70, 94–131, *110*, *112*, 144–5, 147, 151–2
programme music for 100
Going for a Song (book) 129–131
grandchildren, Arthur's 157, 159–161
Grayson, Larry 142
great grandchildren 157

Heal & Sons 85
Hendrie, The (sale at) 64–6

Hepplewhite, George 10, 82, 88
holidays 163–5
Holland-Ford, Robert *55*, 105
Howe, Pamela *52*, 101

Inchbald, Jacqueline *50*
Irving, John *51*, 9, 133

Kent, William 82
Kiddell, James 96–7
King, John *51*, 100
King's Road, Reading 12, *45*
knockers 89–92

Lanning, Mary *52*
literary lunches *115*, 132
Llangattock Book of Hours 66
Lord's Taverners, the 147–8

Makepiece, John 84
Marks, Alfred *112*
Marshall, Arthur 150
Mellon, Paul 27
Minster Street, Reading 12
Montague, Lord 70
More, Kenneth *115*
Morecombe, Eric 147–8

Negus, a 138
Negus, Anne (daughter) 34–5, 39, 157–8
Negus, Arthur G. (Arthur's father) 12–16, 18, *45*, 153–4
Negus, Hilary (daughter) 33–4, 39, 155, 156–7
Negus, Mrs (Arthur's mother) 15, 19, 33
Negus, Mrs (Arthur's wife) *see* Queenie
Negus Enjoys 59, 142
Norden, Denis 132
Norfolk, Duke of 152
Northumberland, Duke of *52*

Nyman, Ben 25–9

Oeben, Jean-François *57*
O'Neill, Captain Terence 108
On the Road 135–40
Osterley House 140
Ottery St Mary *59*

painting, views on 164
pâte-sur-pâte 25, 27
Penn, William, bust of 31–2
Perth *110*
Pitt, Sarah 101
police, Arthur's work with 40–44
press, interviews with the 150
Price, Bernard *51, 52,* 101–2, *114, 121,* 151
Pride of Place 52, 133–4
public, relations with 102–3, 148–9

Queenie 15–16, 33, 37, 44, 106–7, *120,* 129, 130–1, 155, 156, 157, 159, 161

Ravenscroft, George 21
Reading Fine Art Galleries 37–8, 42
Reading School *48*
Reardon, Ray *59,* 142
Rippon, Angela *110*
Robertson, Max *50, 51,* 95, 98–9, *110, 112,* 126, 147
Russell, Gordon 85

St Mary's Church, Reading 16, 22–3, 33, *46*
school and schooldays 12, 14, 16–17, 165
Scully, Hugh *52,* 100, *114*
sculptures, story of the stolen 92–3
Sheraton, Thomas 88
Silver's 12
Sinden, Donald *50*

Solon, Marc Louis 25
Staal, Charlie 65
stone lions, story of 23–4
Stormont, visit to 108–9
Story of English Furniture, The 146–7
Syon House *52,* 140–1

Talking about Antiques 51, 52, 100–102, *114,* 130–1
talking pictures 13
Thompson, Julian *112*

Van, Geoffry *50*
Vandekar, Earl 96
Van Eyck, Jan 66
Vile, William *57*

War effort, Arthur's involvement in 39–43
Wimbledon, visits to 36–7
Wheeler, Sir Mortimer 106–107
Whittaker, Roger 97

Acknowledgments

The photograph on page 57 is reproduced by Gracious Permission of Her Majesty The Queen.
Associated Newspapers, London 45; Author 120; Berkshire County Library, Reading 47; Birmingham Post & Mail 115 top; BBC, London 50 top, 50 bottom, 51 top, 51 bottom, 52 top, 52 bottom, 55, 109, 110 top, 111 bottom, 112, 113, 114 top, 114 bottom, 115 bottom; Camera Press, London 116–117, 122–123; Christie's, London 56 top, 56 bottom; City of Gloucester 49 top; Evening Post, Jersey 124; C Finden, Reading 49 bottom; John Frost, Newcastle 121; Gloucestershire Gazette: D Ireland 119; P M Hatch, Reading 48; Illustrated London News: Neil Libbert 53; Radio Times, London 54, 110 bottom; Reading Museum and Art Gallery 46; Syndication International, London 60, 118; D C Thomson, Dundee 111 top; Western Morning News, Plymouth 58, 59